TREASURE
FOR THE
NATION

CONSERVING OUR HERITAGE

TREASURES
FOR THE
NATION
CONSERVING OUR HERITAGE

Published by British Museum Publications
for the National Heritage Memorial Fund

Exhibition sponsored by

British Gas

British Library Cataloguing in Publication Data
National Heritage Memorial Fund.
Treasures for the nation.
1. Great Britain. National Heritage
Memorial Fund, Art objects. Catalogues,
indexes
I. Title
709'.03

ISBN 0-7141-1665-3

Exhibition dates: 27 October 1988 to 26 February 1989

Exhibition Organisers: Anne Seymour and Caroline Chapman

Edited by Suzannah Gough
Designed by Behram Kapadia
Set in Linotron Bembo by Rowland Phototypesetting Ltd
Bury St Edmunds, Suffolk and printed in Great Britain
by Lund Humphries, London and Bradford

Front cover: (Detail) The 'Southampton Armour'. No. 3
Back cover: *The Concert* Hendrick ter Brugghen. No. 30
Frontispiece: (Detail). Beilby Goblet. No. 58.
Title-page: The Mostyn Tompion Clock. No. 51

CONTENTS

Acknowledgements

We would like to thank the many people who have given so much advice and support to the Exhibition. We are particularly grateful to Colin Amery, and our Advisory Panel:

Marcus Binney, Claude Blair, Alan Borg, Tim Burnett, Christopher Gilbert, Gervase Jackson-Stops, Brian Lacey, Brian Lang, David Learmont, Richard Ormond, David Sekers, Neil Stratford, Dr Christopher Thacker, David Tomlinson, Giles Waterfield.

We should also like to thank Diana Berry and Alan Dodd.

We are very grateful to the lenders for writing the catalogue entries and the following:

M. M. Archibald no. 24; Iain Bain no. 67; Professor Rosemary Cramp no. 19; David Francis no. 101, 116; Christopher Gilbert (and the National Trust) no. 92, 92a, b, c, d, e; Ian Lyle no. 69; Sir Oliver Millar no. 88; Francis Russell no. 93; David Sekers no. 110; Dr Christopher Thacker no. 72 (introduction), 73 (and the National Trust), 74, 75, 76 and L. E. Webster no. 24.

The catalogue was compiled by Anne Seymour.

Aberglaslyn, Gwynedd, Wales. *The National Trust.*

Sponsor's Foreword

British Gas is delighted to sponsor *Treasures for the Nation*. It is a great privilege to help make possible such an important event, and we are glad to have this opportunity to express our support for the National Heritage Memorial Fund and the valuable work it is doing.

This exhibition has a message for us all. We live in a rapidly changing world where our national heritage is constantly under threat. It is our hope that *Treasures for the Nation* will lead to greater public appreciation of what is meant by the nation's heritage. Visitors to this exhibition will see the achievements of Britain's engineers in their rightful place alongside the work of her artists, while the beauty and fragility of the countryside is also emphasised.

Above all *Treasures for the Nation* is of immense educational importance. It helps young and old alike to appreciate the lasting value that comes from the pursuit of excellence by the artist or engineer. It also provides a reaffirmation of the richness and variety of those things, created by man and nature, which make up the fabric of our nation.

British Gas too is part of that fabric. Because our activities touch the lives of so many people, we believe that we have a wider responsibility to the community we serve. We demonstrate that commitment in our care for the environment, through our support for education, and in our sponsorship of events such as this.

British Gas hopes that visitors to the British Museum will find *Treasures for the Nation* a rewarding and enriching experience.

Sir Denis Rooke CBE FRS FEng
Chairman
British Gas

Preface

All who pay taxes should know how their pennies get spent.

The central purpose of this exhibition is to show the public how, during the first years of its existence, the National Heritage Memorial Fund has spent tax payers' money, entrusted to it by Her Majesty's Government, for the defence of our National Heritage.

There are two other purposes: one is to give pleasure for there is much of beauty and interest to be seen, and the other is to sound a warning that the National Heritage in all its aspects remains under constant threat.

The first annual report of the Fund, that for 1980–81, began with words written in 1587, by Sir Francis Drake: 'There must be a beginning to any great matter but the continuing unto the end, until it be thoroughly finished yields the true glory'. We went on to say that the 'great matter' of saving the Heritage would never be thoroughly finished, but we looked forward instead to a voyage of mercy with many ports of call. This exhibition shows something of the splendour and variety of what we have so far been able to save for the nation on our journey.

The museum objects – the paintings, the sculpture and the furniture – speak for themselves but what can not be so easily illustrated, and what must depend for their exposition on photographs and videos are the great country houses with their contents and their gardens, and the woodland, wetland, and wilderness which have also been preserved.

At the time the exhibition opens we shall have spent nearly £100 million, and without that expenditure a very great deal of what is on show and much more for which there is no space, would have been lost. We believe that what we have been able to do has been extremely worthwhile, and we are infinitely grateful to Her Majesty's Government for the manner in which they have sustained us.

In all their deliberations the Trustees have remembered that the Fund was established by Parliament, in succession to the National Land Fund to be 'a memorial to those who have died for the United Kingdom'. Some of the exhibits, such as the World War I Tank outside the Museum, specifically reflect this purpose.

The Trustees of the National Heritage Memorial Fund are particularly grateful to British Gas for their sponsorship of this Exhibition. Without their generous help and ready co-operation it could never have been mounted. Their thanks also go to all those who have generously lent the pictures and objects.

Finally, they are deeply grateful to the Trustees and Director of the British Museum for generously allowing the exhibition to be held in the Museum's magnificent galleries, and to their staff for the advice and expertise which they have lavished on it.

Lord Charteris of Amisfield
Chairman
National Heritage Memorial Fund

Measurements of paintings are given as: height × width

Exhibitions mentioned in the catalogue are since NHMF has given a grant

Abbreviations:

NA-CF	National Art-Collections Fund
RSPB	Royal Society for the Protection of Birds
RCHM	Royal Commission on the Historic Monuments of England
MGC/V&A	Purchase grant fund administered by the Victoria and Albert Museum on behalf of the Museums and Galleries Commission
LMPF	Local Museums Purchase Fund

INTRODUCTION

Bluebird, 1961; no. 2.

The National Heritage: the development of an idea since 1870

JOHN CORNFORTH

Names, words and phrases tend to develop a sense of period: this is certainly so of the term, the National Heritage, which now has a ring of the mid and late 1970s about it. The term was first most frequently heard in the campaign to protect historic houses, their collections and settings when these were threatened by Wealth Tax and Capital Transfer Tax in 1974. The term itself embodies a very English sense of property as a trust, which the country house has always been, and so the term was coined by those concerned to see houses and their collections preserved for posterity. From the specific application of the National Heritage to historic houses and their collections, the use of the term has since been extended to cover almost every aspect of the fabric of British life that is felt worth handing on to posterity: not just historic houses, but all kinds of buildings, landscapes and coastlines, as well as works of art and the visual and documentary evidence of political, social and industrial history.

When the National Heritage Memorial Fund was established in 1980 its brief was left intentionally vague so that the Trustees could exercise their own judgement about what was and what was not part of the national heritage. Consequently, when recently I read a leader in *Country Life* published as long ago as 25 January 1930 entitled *The National Heritage*, it made me think about the development of the concept during the last one hundred years. The stages through which the concept of national heritage passed are familiar enough, but the steady alteration of the balance between public interest and private property rights would not, of itself, account for the dramatically changed attitude of the Government that lies at the heart of the matter. When the first National Monuments Bill was introduced in 1873 it was seen as an attack on private property rights, and, when it was finally passed in 1882, it was a very mild measure, listing only sixty-eight monuments that could be taken into guardianship if their owners consented. The year 1882, it must be remembered, was also the year of the Settled Estates Act, which gave tenants for life the power to sell land.

The influence of John Ruskin and William Morris led to the establishment of various preservation societies: first the Commons Preservation Society in 1865, the Society for the Protection of Ancient Buildings in 1877, the National Footpaths Preservation Society in 1884, the National Trust in 1895 and the National Art-Collections Fund in 1903. By the late nineteenth century not only were urban pressures on the countryside building up, but the effects of agricultural depression seemed to be very seriously compounded by the introduction of death duties in 1894. However the first signs of 'heritage' thinking appeared almost immediately, with the exemption of works of art in 1896. The year 1907 saw the first National Trust Act and the establishment of the Royal Commission on Historical Monuments.

Although there was a growing awareness and nostalgia for Britain's past, preservation, however, was still very much a private activity. The Government did little, not taking into guardianship a single monument in the first thirty years after

Detail of *Landscape with the Ashes of Phocion* by Nicolas Poussin; no. 38.

the passing of the first Act. The hopelessness of the official system became obvious in 1911 with the threat to Tattershall Castle, which was finally averted by Lord Curzon. That led to the 1913 Act introducing the concept of preservation orders.

Despite the admiration that developed in the 1890s for the architecture of Wren and his period, the RCHM's brief ended at 1700 and it concentrated on the period before 1600. Earthworks, crucks and gables were in; porticoes were out. The work of Robert Adam, despite the Adams Revival of the 1880s and 1890s, was still not admired in the reign of Edward VII. British classical architecture only began to be considered seriously just before the First World War, when A.E. Richardson published his *Monumental Classic Architecture in Great Britain and Ireland*, taking the story down to 1880. Boulton's book on Adam, advertised as being in the press in 1914, did not appear until 1922, and Country Life's *English Homes* series, which began in 1920, reached *Late Georgian* in 1926 and *Vanbrugh* in 1928. By 1930 Georgian houses were fashionable, but Victorian architecture was out, and with it the work of Webb and Shaw who had been admired in the first decade of the century. Only to Evelyn Waugh in *A Handful of Dust* (1934) and a few others was its future return to favour clear.

This broadening of the historical perspective was essential to the development of the concept recognised today as the national heritage, but even after the First World War, when huge land sales were resumed, there was remarkably little feeling that any official action could or should be taken to save historic houses.

By 1928, when Christopher Hussey wrote about Dorchester House, Park Lane, attitudes were changing, and the threat to the house stimulated a considerable effort for preservation. Hussey wrote: 'A country that lives on capital, treating death duties as income, must not expect monuments of individualism to survive.' Seven years later, when Bramshill was put up for sale, he wrote even more strongly: 'It has been, and should in a rightly ordered world continue to be, a national possession; . . . Rumours have indeed been current that the State contemplates its purchase intact for preservation.' The previous year Lord Lothian had made a speech to the National Trust's Annual Meeting that prompted it to formulate its Country Houses Scheme; and the first major bequest under it was that of Blickling by Lord Lothian in 1940.

The late 1920s to the mid 1930s were the key years for concern about the preservation of country houses. For the first time enthusiasm and knowledge joined forces with economic pressures. Lord Lothian's speech is rightly seen as a landmark, but in fact it was well timed rather than a bolt from the blue. In 1932 R.C. Norman, who was a banker, refused to accept the chairmanship of the National Trust because he foresaw the time when the Trust would be offered great estates and he believed that the chairman ought to be a landowner. There was, moreover, not only a new appreciation of eighteenth-century architecture but also of eighteenth-century landscape, and here again aesthetics and enthusiasm joined forces with new pressures, pressures that were urban and suburban as well as economic. In 1927 Christopher Hussey wrote *The Picturesque*, which, although primarily a study of the past, was also a primer for the present.

Here it is worth quoting from the *Country Life* leader of 1930, *The National Heritage*: 'A great deal of rural beauty of this country we owe to the enterprise and love of nature of past landowners. That our great country houses, with their treasures of art, their wide-spreading parks and delightful gardens, have now come to be considered as national and not merely personal heritages we owe to the generosity and practical public spirit of the landowners of to-day.' The leader goes on to say that such generosity could not be extended indefinitely and to ask the Government to extend exemption on works of art to houses, parks and woods open for public enjoyment.

It was not just the rural face of England that was being transformed by new roads, houses and factories, but also the urban face. The west end of London was under particular pressure, and one by one the great houses were going. However, the scheme in 1932 to rebuild Carlton House Terrace and replace it with new buildings by Sir Reginald Blomfield prompted an outcry on a new scale. That storm marked what was to become a key element in the rise of preservation thinking, a marked hostility to the new and the 'Modern'. It took a long time for the Modern Movement to make a physical impression in Britain, but it is interesting to note that by 1931 Christopher Hussey was worried about the effect of the new architecture on the landscape.

The outbreak of the Second World War had a two-edged effect: it delayed activity, but at the same time it was taken as an opportunity for creative thought about planning and preservation that bore fruit after 1945. The establishment of The National Monuments Record, for instance, was a response to threats of destruction by bombing and afterwards it became the foundation for the listing of historic buildings. The war also saw the steady growth of the National Trust's Country Houses Scheme.

Peace in 1945 brought three major benefits: first, the determination of returning owners of great houses to get them going again; second, the idea of the National Land Fund, a concept based on ideals about public benefit that had been developed during the previous half century but which, unfortunately, had been later betrayed by politicians; and third, the introduction of repair grants for historic buildings in 1953. Thus in the years 1945 to 1953 concerns that had been felt before the war became the basis of a new system founded on the acceptance of the idea that the Government had a positive role to play.

At first thinking was no doubt inspired by a view of the history of architecture that ended about 1830, but very soon it began to be affected by the rediscovery of the Victorian period. A little later this rediscovery came to embrace achievements of the Industrial Revolution in engineering, technology and transport just at a time when fundamental changes in older British industries threatened a whole range of structures and machines that had hitherto been taken for granted. There also developed a new interest in social history. Together they were to have a profound effect on attitudes to conservation: not only on the question of what should be conserved, but also on who should be responsible for conservation and how it should be carried out.

The titles of certain books demonstrate the early stages of this enthusiasm for conservation: *Art and the Industrial Revolution* by Francis Klingender (1947), *Pioneers of Modern Design* by Nikolaus Pevsner (1949), and *Early Victorian Architecture in Britain* by Henry Russell Hitchcock (1954). The term Industrial Archaeology was apparently only introduced in 1955. When the Victorian Society was formed in 1958 it faced a broader challenge than that facing the Georgian Group in 1937; and its battle over the Euston Arch in 1962 did a great deal to widen the base of preservation both in terms of causes and supporters. Already thoughts were turning to the positive preservation of industrial sites. In 1959, for instance, to mark the preservation of the foundation of the Coalbrookdale Company, the old Darby furnace at Coalbrookdale was repaired and opened as a site.

The broadening of the concept of the heritage is not just an expansion of historical enthusiasms. It is also an administrative device used by Government to tidy into one field a whole range of problems from a number of different departments that were seldom individually expensive but which were time-consuming and difficult to handle. For Government it is much easier to give insufficient but regular help to an arm's-length body and leave it to make the decisions; what is interesting is that the establishment of the NHMF has caused the concept of the National Heritage to move constantly forward.

Detail of *The Virgin and Child with Angels*
by Joos van Cleve; no. 36.

The Albatross and the Phoenix: the fate of great houses

MARCUS BINNEY

'Hardly a week passes when one does not see the auctioneer's notice of the impending sale and dissolution of some big estate. The house is seized by the demolition contractors, its park invaded and churned up by the timber merchant. Down comes the house; down come the tall trees, naked and gashed lies the once-beautiful park.' These lines, and there were more in the same angry, despairing vein, were not written by an impassioned architectural historian or country house enthusiast but come as the climax of W.G. Hoskins's magisterial survey of the face of England from prehistoric times. *The Making of the English Landscape* was first published in 1955, the year which marked the nadir of the country house.

For the exhibition *The Destruction of the Country House* at the Victoria and Albert Museum, London, in October 1974, John Harris set out to compile a list of all the country houses demolished in Britain since 1870. Thanks to the painstaking researches of Derek Sherborne and Peter Reid, the total reached the devastating figure of 1,500. Little was recorded about many of these houses; photographs of several hundred of them were assembled using the resources of The National Monuments Record in London, old postcards and family photograph albums; and particulars were ferreted out from estate agents and demolition contractors. When the annual losses came to be counted, one year stood out: 1955. In that year no fewer than seventy-five notable country houses had been lost, and that was the year in which Professor Hoskins's searing words were published.

In no other European country were large country houses demolished in such numbers, and this was because the listing of historic buildings only began in Britain in 1946. Many of the country houses demolished in the late 1940s and 1950s disappeared long before the ministry investigators reached the area in which they stood, and even if they were listed, the legislation was too feeble to prevent demolition.

And yet, the means existed to save at least some of them, for in the 1946 Budget, the Chancellor of the Exchequer, Dr Hugh Dalton, had established a National Land Fund, with an initial grant of £50 m (a large enough sum today but enormous then) intended to bring a whole range of property into public hands. Dr Dalton was concerned that the Inland Revenue was consistently failing to make use of provisions in the 1910 Finance Act which enable death duties to be satisfied by handing over property instead of cash.

In one of the most rousing speeches ever delivered in Parliament on the nation's heritage Dalton concluded: 'It is surely fitting in this proud moment of our history, when we are celebrating victory and deliverance from overwhelming evils and horrors that we should make, through this Fund, a thank-offering for victory, and a war-memorial which many would think finer than any work of art in stone or bronze. I should like to think that, through this Fund, we shall dedicate some of the loveliest parts of this land to the memory of those who died that we might live in freedom.'

Sofa by John Linnell from the State Drawing Room, Kedleston Hall; no. 87c.

The National Land Fund had been created in the teeth of Treasury opposition. The money was simply invested in Treasury Stock and left to be spent, or rather not spent, on the recommendation of Treasury officials. The Fund was largely forgotten, though in 1953 and 1956 its scope had been broadened to include works of art as well as land and buildings. By 1957 it had risen, despite some expenditure on significant properties, from £50 m to £60 m.

But, in that year the Fund, the nation's war memorial, was ruthlessly plundered, axed by £50 m, exactly the amount Parliament had originally voted. Even with this, substantial acquisitions were made: money from the National Land Fund enabled Hardwick, Saltram, Shugborough and Sudbury to be accepted in payment of death duties and handed to the National Trust.

These great houses presented one serious problem for the National Trust: they came without endowment. As a result there was a substantial deficit on running costs. Although successive governments met these deficits with Historic Buildings Council grants, the National Trust understandably grew disenchanted with payment in arrears and by the end of the 1960s the Trust was refusing to accept more houses in this way without endowment.

The case that brought the issue to a head was Heveningham Hall in Suffolk. This palatial house, looking down to a beautiful 'Capability' Brown lake, was trapped in a discretionary trust, under which Capital Gains Tax became payable every fifteen years on all the assets of the Trust whether or not they were sold. Somewhat unwillingly the Government bought the house, many of the original contents and 400 acres for £303,662. But this time the National Trust firmly refused to take on the house without an endowment, and although it did later agree to run the house on a temporary basis, to the civil servants this was untidy, and increasingly they saw the purchase of Heveningham as a mistake.

So when the great Rothschild house at Mentmore was offered to the Government as part of a death duty package the response was less than lukewarm. Once again the initial asking price of £2 m for house, principal contents and parkland seems in retrospect an amazing bargain. But this was a time of stringent controls over public expenditure, and Ministers decided to seek a private commercial sponsor. Negotiations were kept secret, and when Lord Rosebery's offer lapsed after more than a year of fruitless negotiations no one could ascertain whether the commercial sponsor had been a serious possibility or not.

At Save Britain's Heritage our fury was intense. Within a week, in 1977 we produced a leaflet, *SAVE Mentmore for the Nation*, illustrating the house for the first time. As the campaign developed our attention turned to the National Land Fund, and we found that the money was there, standing at £17,524,799 on 31 March 1976. By this time it had lost all independence, but £1 m was allocated from it to the Department of the Environment for the purchase of historic buildings, and £1 m to the Office of Arts and Libraries for the acquisition of works of art for public collections. The two departments together had the sum needed to purchase Mentmore and its treasures, but we were told that it could not be done. In the months leading up to the Sotheby's sale we taunted the Government daily with the absurdity of the situation, calculating that the acquisition of just some of Mentmore's treasures for national museums would cost at least £1 m.

The public outcry resulted in the Environment Committee of the House of Commons reporting on the National Land Fund. Two main recommendations were made: the National Land Fund should be re-established with independent Trustees as the National Heritage Memorial Fund; and the Fund should have powers to make endowments. The National Heritage Act, 1980, enshrined these recommendations, and the system began to work. The first rescue operation was for Canons Ashby in Northamptonshire, where the garden had been left to run wild. Initiatives could now be taken outside Whitehall and with the help of the Heritage Fund a National Trust rescue package was put together.

Within months, three great houses were threatened with break-up almost simultaneously. Belton House in Lincolnshire, perhaps the most perfect Charles II house in England, was followed by Calke Abbey in Derbyshire, a time capsule where nothing had ever been thrown away, and finally by Fyvie in Aberdeenshire, a prodigy house with a magnificent collection of portraits. The sums involved were enormous: some £9 m for Belton, £4.5 m for Calke Abbey, and £3 m for Fyvie. And to its great credit the Government provided, in 1985, a further £25 m for the Fund to resolve the future of three further great houses: Robert Adam's Kedleston Hall in Derbyshire, Nostell Priory in Yorkshire, another great Adam house, and Weston Park in Staffordshire.

Public patronage has, however, been more than matched by private generosity. In these years the National Trust received a series of great houses with contents, land to protect and investments to endow them, including Erddig in Wales, Basildon Park in Berkshire, and Wimpole Hall in Cambridgeshire. In 1982 the Trust received Kingston Lacy, and in Scotland Hopetoun House was vested in a private charitable trust, while Leeds Castle in Kent was left by Lady Baillie with an endowment of £6 m as a charitable trust dedicated to the cause of medical research and education; and in the greatest gesture of all, the Duke of Devonshire placed Chatsworth and its treasures in a charitable trust for one hundred years.

The great virtue of the NHMF is its willingness to tackle the really large problem houses, and the run of successes was to be broken by Monkton, the surrealist fantasy created by Edward James. Expert opinion was divided on the merits of Monkton, and, alas, the NHMF Trustees decided against rescuing the house.

And yet, no one knows which great house will be the next to face a crisis, or when. The success of the NHMF has been due to the Government's willingness to respond quickly when problems arise. The Fund should be truly independent, but it is in reality dependent on what the Government provides year by year, or by way of special bounty. There may be no prospect of the Government returning the £50 m taken from the National Land Fund in 1957, but the NHMF has shown initiative and judgement that deserves more than the uncertainty of an unpredictable annual grant. The time has come for the Government to look ahead not one year only but at least five.

Moon Ponds and the Temple of Piety, Studley Royal; no. 75.

The National Heritage Memorial Fund: a continuing role

BRIAN LANG

It is almost a maxim that we do not realise how much we care for something until we are about to lose it. So it is with our national heritage.

The countryside in Britain is being changed in ways and at a speed that threatens to make it unrecognisable in a few years. Hedgerows disappear as the familiar patchwork of small fields becomes vast prairies suitable for more highly mechanised farming. Swathes of conifers are planted over open moorland. Wetlands are drained with dire effects on wildlife. Great historic houses risk losing their contents – furniture, works of art, and other items collected over generations which give such houses much of their personality – as their owners find the cost of maintenance too great. Important works of art fetch sums on the open market which few buyers in this country can match. Monuments to our industrial past – the water-powered cotton mills and early iron foundries on which Britain's wealth was once based – need sympathetic owners with the imagination and entrepreneurial flair to ensure that these frequently vast buildings can face safe futures with appropriate new uses.

It may be, however, that we are realising the value of what we have lost or are about to lose in the nick of time. Interest in conservation in the United Kingdom is now very great and 'the national heritage', its care, maintenance, and its employment as a leisure pursuit, is a growing industry. In 1987 the National Trust had over 1.5 million members, and over 8.5 million paid visits were made to National Trust properties. The Royal Society for the Protection of Birds has half a million members and an annual income of over £10 m. It was not always thus. The tremendous growth of such organisations has been the result of an upsurge of interest in the national heritage, and of an awareness of the dangers facing the heritage.

The Government decided, in the aftermath of the dispersal of Mentmore's contents in 1977, that a new mechanism was needed to deal with national heritage emergencies. The National Heritage Memorial Fund was created in 1980 as a 'fire engine' for the heritage. It steps in at times of crisis, when an important item is in grave danger of imminent loss, by export, dilapidation or irreversible damage. The NHMF decides on the basis of requests from conservation bodies whether or not to give assistance to save a particular item for the national heritage.

The NHMF is government-funded, and is run by up to eleven Trustees appointed by the Prime Minister. Its task, quoting from the National Heritage Act, 1980, is to give financial assistance towards the acquisition, preservation or maintenance of 'any land, building or structure which in the opinion of the Trustees is of outstanding scenic, historic, aesthetic, architectural or scientific interest' and which is also 'of importance to the national heritage'.

No definition of 'the national heritage' was provided to the NHMF, and its Trustees decided to attempt no such definition in the belief that this could only be as artificial or limited as a definition of, say, 'art' or 'beauty'. The Chairman of Trustees, therefore, is likely to lead his colleagues through an agenda which would in other circumstances seem of bewildering variety. A typical monthly meeting

Osprey at Loch Garten reserve in Invernesshire, Scotland. A grant from the Fund to the RSPB has safeguarded this breeding area. From the original pair at Loch Garten the population of ospreys in Scotland now numbers almost 50 pairs.

might require decisions on a painting by a Dutchman, a piece of English furniture, a breeding area for black grouse, a 1930s aeroplane and a film made by Laurence Olivier in 1944. Fresh developments in negotiations over one or two large country houses might be reported. All of these the Trustees now take in their stride as constituent parts of the national heritage. The NHMF is continually defining the national heritage in a 'naming of parts' process.

Until the creation of the NHMF, no national body had existed which had responsibility for such a wide range of items. Other bodies such as the National Trust, the Historic Buildings Council, museums, the Countryside Commission or the Royal Society for the Protection of Birds all do indispensable work in their particular areas of interest. With the arrival of the NHMF and the desire of its Trustees to regard their remit as wide and as flexible as possible, there now exists a single organisation which can make judgements about the countryside, works of art, wildlife and steam locomotives within the same terms of reference. The national heritage is now a seamless robe.

But why bother to save it? Does economic development not make memories of the past increasingly redundant? By spending public money on works of art by long-dead artists, on centuries-old buildings and stretches of open countryside, are we not diverting resources from the encouragement of living artists, stifling appreciation of modern architecture, preventing economic development in rural areas? An obvious answer to such criticism has already been referred to above: the

The Portland Font; no. 54.

tremendous surge in public enthusiasm and support for the idea of conservation. A further answer lies in the notion of 'conserving'. We are not merely preserving. If to preserve is simply to keep in existence, to conserve an object is to do much more than that. The conservation process is about giving new roles to things from the past. A historic house may be opened to the public, a dockside warehouse converted into flats, an area of countryside protected so that it is available for activities additional to simply 'economic development'. To conserve the national heritage is to make the best of what we already possess, to nurture it and to give it a role from which public benefit will flow. Conservation is at the same time about protection of those items we most cherish, and ensuring that they have real uses, be these educational, economic or life-enhancing.

   That we concentrate on 'the best' is partly a result of scarce financial resources. Money for conservation projects is limited and so can be provided only for the most important ones. The NHMF turns down approximately four projects for every one it agrees to support, usually because the item is of insufficient importance to the national heritage, or because it does not represent good value for money. An item may be conserved because, more straightforwardly, it makes this country a more pleasant place in which to live. Conservation is an activity which seeks constantly to maintain and improve the quality of life in Britain. A painting may, quite simply, be beautiful to behold; an area of moorland in its natural state may be enjoyable to walk across; the ingenuity of a steam engine may give great pleasure simply in its continuing operation. In terms of the economy, the heritage now plays a vital role in a tourist industry worth £13 billion a year.

The judgements made by the NHMF about which projects to support, and those which are not felt worthy of support, can be very difficult. Not everyone will agree with the Trustees on every occasion. What is certain, though, is that the national heritage will continue for the foreseeable future to need rescue operations on a scale which will require Government intervention. Mechanisms for such action exist in agencies such as the NHMF, English Heritage and the Historic Buildings Council as well as through the availability of indirect support such as tax concessions and mechanisms for the acceptance of heritage property.

This Government has a record in the field of conservation which is admired by many other countries. This does not mean, though, that the NHMF has enjoyed an easy ride. The Fund has been on a financial tightrope ever since its inception. Since 1980 it has spent nearly £100 m in saving for the nation a vast array of buildings, works of art, areas of landscape and other items which, but for NHMF intervention, would most likely have been lost. Annual expenditure rose from £2.5 m in the first year to almost £40 m in 1986–7. While resources have been made available by Government to meet such expenditure, funding has not been on a basis of regular annual grants such as have permitted clear-sighted forward planning and the setting of priorities. Regular grants have been modest, to say the least, while the Fund's major spending needs have been met from often substantial end-of-year grants when the government has found itself with spare cash from its own underspending. These end-of-year handouts have on occasions been large: £25 m in 1985 and £20 m in 1987. But this kind of bailing-out can be no substitute for regular, budgeted income from Government, and it is high time that Government committed itself to providing regular grants which match the NHMF's needs.

The NHMF still has a continuingly vital role to fulfil. The national heritage does not represent a passive memory of the past; it is a living, useful force, neither parochial nor narrow. It includes works of art by foreign artists as well as Edwardian fairground roundabouts. These are treasures from a national past. Unless we take active steps to protect them, they could all, very easily, disappear forever. There are few second chances in conservation.

CATALOGUE

The Memorial Aspect

ALAN BORG

There shall be a fund known as the National Heritage Memorial Fund, to be a memorial to those who have died for the United Kingdom.

(National Heritage Act, 1980)

Wars have been fought since the dawn of humanity, and from antiquity memorials have been made to commemorate those who have died in battle. From the Great Mound at Marathon to the Cenotaph in London, the world is littered with memorials to those who died in the incongruous folly of war, an activity which degrades humanity in general while at the same time inspiring individuals to acts of exceptional bravery and self-sacrifice.

Memorials fall into two groups, which may be termed active and passive. The majority are passive, having no purpose but to remind us of what they commemorate. The public monuments we normally think of as war memorials, in town squares or on village greens, fall into this category. The First World War was followed by an unprecedented period of memorial construction, the results of which were dependent upon a long tradition of memorial iconography, including classical allegories of victory and peace together with Christian symbolism.

From the beginning, however, some have felt that such passive memorials were insufficient, that the memory of the dead should be commemorated in a more positive way. The result has been a second category of memorials, active ones, which exist not just to prompt the memory but to provide some actual benefit for those who remain. The earliest such memorials were religious structures, like the Parthenon in Athens or the Great Altar at Pergamon, which recalled in a general sense those who died for their country and thereby allowed the living to acknowledge and celebrate the divine. In the Middle Ages such religious foundations had a more direct role. William the Conqueror founded Battle Abbey as a thank-offering for his victory at Hastings, and sited the high altar on the spot where Harold fell.

Churches and monasteries have an obvious application for the living as well as providing a memorial for the dead, but there was a desire to provide still more practical forms of commemoration. By the nineteenth century this led to the establishment of various charitable funds and charitable institutions, with terms of reference that enshrined the memorial concept. The building of almshouses and hospitals for old soldiers was a popular way of expressing this intention, and a good number of such worthy establishments were set up after the First World War, as an alternative, or in addition, to the passive stone memorials.

After the Second World War there were renewed attempts to create cultural memorials. The inadequacy of the stone memorial was tacitly recognised by the fact that very few new ones were constructed, with the names of those who had given their lives being added instead to the existing First World War memorials. Therefore in 1946 the National Land Fund was established as a memorial, although the concept and uses of this were insufficiently explicit. It was only in 1980 that the Land Fund became the basis of the National Heritage Memorial Fund. By including the words Heritage and Memorial in its title the Fund publicly acknowledged its derivation from the concept of the active memorial.

Lancaster Bombers of No. 44 Squadron, R.A.F., 1942. no. 16.

1

1 *Flirt II*

British, 1917
*The Trustees of the Tank Museum, Bovington, Dorset, and
Lincoln City Council*

Mark IV tanks such as *Flirt II* were built in larger numbers than
any other British tank of the First World War. Approximately
1,200 were produced by a group of engineering firms that
included William Foster & Co. Ltd of Lincoln, builders of the
very first tanks. Both male and female types were made: male
tanks were equipped with six-pounder guns while females
carried machine guns only. Each tank weighed around 28
tons and required a crew of eight to operate it.

Flirt II belonged to F, or 6th Battalion of the Tank Corps,
and is believed to be the only machine to survive from the
Battle of Cambrai. This action, which began on 20 November 1917, was the first in which tanks were used in significant
numbers as the principal arm in battle. It is thus hailed as the
first successful tank battle in which large areas of enemy
territory were taken for only modest casualties among the
infantry.

For many years *Flirt II* stood on a plinth outside the Tank
Museum at Bovington Camp in Dorset, but time and ex-
posure took their toll. Then, in the summer of 1983, an
agreement was reached with the City of Lincoln, for its
long-term loan and restoration. The work was carried out by
a Youth Training Scheme team at Ruston Gas Turbines in the
city.

The NHMF recognised the historic interest of this tank and
its importance to the national heritage, and in 1983 was
delighted to provide a grant of £7,800 for the vital conservation work needed on this and two other important tanks.

2 *Bluebird*

British, 1960, length 9.144 m
*The Trustees of the Science Museum, London, and the Trustees
of the National Motor Museum, Beaulieu, Hampshire*
EXHIBITIONS: *Motorfair*, London, 1983; on tour, Australia,
1985

Donald Campbell, son of the illustrious Malcolm Campbell,
masterminded this *Bluebird* which was completed by the
Norris brothers of Burgess Hill in the summer of 1960. It is
powered by a Bristol-Siddeley Proteus gas turbine engine
which gave about 4,100 h.p. at 11,000 r.p.m. and drove all
four wheels. The car, which is 9 metres long, weighs more
than 4 tons. Its construction was a communal effort between
about seventy British component manufacturing firms; some
of the most prominent were British Petroleum who provided
substantial backing, Dunlop who developed completely
new wheels and tyres, Bristol-Siddeley who provided and
modified the power unit, and Motor Panels Limited who
constructed the body.

Donald Campbell's first record attempt was made in
August 1960 at Bonneville Salt Flats, Utah, and ended in
disaster with a serious crash. *Bluebird* was then rebuilt with a
large stabilising tail fin which it still carries, and further
attempts were made on the record at Lake Eyre in Australia.
Campbell was finally rewarded on 17 July 1964 when he
achieved a speed of 403.10 m.p.h., beating the previous
record set up by John Cobb by nearly 9 m.p.h.

In 1972 *Bluebird* was loaned to the National Motor Museum
at Beaulieu and in 1981 Tonia Campbell, widow of the late
Donald Campbell, decided to sell the car. On 18 September
1981 it was announced that *Bluebird* had been bought for the

2. Illustrated in colour on p. 11

nation for £85,000. The majority of the money (£63,750) had come from the NHMF, with contributions from the National Motor Museum and the Science Museum in London. The car was to be the property of the Science Museum and a condition of its purchase was that it was to remain on indefinite loan to the National Motor Museum at Beaulieu.

3   Three-quarter armour for the field

Probably French, c. 1595–1600, etched and gilt-steel
The Trustees of the Royal Armouries, HM Tower of London
II. 360

The armour, made for Henry Wriothesley, 3rd Earl of Southampton (1573–1624), is etched and gilt with an overall design of interlacing snakes amidst foliage populated by grotesques, including birds, insects, snails (some winged) and mammals.

The armour is displayed on a carved wooden stand, decorated with motifs adapted from the decoration of the armour, employing the intertwined snakes as a central medallion within a strapwork panel, surrounded by grotesques. It was probably made for the armour in the late nineteenth century, and it is likely that the restorations to the armour, for example the snake buckles, piccadills and gauntlet linings, were produced at the same time.

The armour appears in a portrait of Southampton, on loan to the National Portrait Gallery at Montacute House from the trustees of the late Duke of Portland, in which the Earl is depicted wearing the collar, with the cuirass on the floor at his feet and the close helmet, plumed, on a plinth beside him. It is thought to have been painted c. 1595–1600, before he was

3

imprisoned in the Tower (1601–3) by Queen Elizabeth I, then freed and created a Knight of the Garter by King James I in 1603.

Southampton was a great scholar and lover of the arts, and is best known as the only patron ever acknowledged by Shakespeare. He served with Essex at Cadiz, in Ireland and in the Low Countries (1596–1600), and may have acquired the armour during a diplomatic mission to Paris in 1598.

The armour was preserved until 1983 in the collection of Lord Astor of Hever at Hever Castle, having been purchased in 1907 from the dealer, Robert Patridge of St James's, London. The armour was sold at Sotheby's in 1983, and, following the suspension of an export licence, a public appeal was launched, to which thousands of individuals and many institutions, including the NHMF, the NA-CF and Sir Emmanuel Kaye, generously contributed. At the eleventh hour the purchase price of £367,000, to which the NHMF contributed £186,475, was raised. The armour has been on display ever since.

4   The Loch Ness Wellington bomber

Built by VICKERS-ARMSTRONG
Weybridge, Surrey, November 1939
Brooklands Museum, Weybridge, Surrey
N 2980

The *Wimpy* was RAF Bomber Command's mainstay during the early years of the Second World War. Its unique geodetic construction, the brainchild of the legendary Barnes Wallis, enabled it to withstand battle damage that would have destroyed lesser machines.

Although built in greater numbers than any other British bomber (11,461), it was thought in 1976 that not a single one that had seen action during the Second World War had survived. In that year a team of American 'monster hunters' picked up on their sonar what they thought was the wreck of a Catalina flying boat lying at the bottom of Loch Ness. A group of researchers from Heriot-Watt University in Edinburgh subsequently surveyed this wreck in 1978 using special underwater television cameras and identified it as an intact and perfectly preserved Wellington bomber. Records revealed that it was a very early Mk I A, number N 2980, that had ditched on Loch Ness on New Year's Eve 1940 due to engine failure. Further research into Air Ministry records uncovered the fact that it was also a survivor of the famous Battle of Heligoland Bight of 18 December 1939. It was this raid that forced Bomber Command to abandon its pre-war policy of daylight precision raids and switch to night-time operations.

Recognising the historical significance of N 2980, the Loch Ness Wellington Association was formed to recover the aircraft and present it to a suitable museum. On 21 September 1985 N 2980's starboard wing tip broke the surface of Loch Ness after forty-five years. The NHMF provided £25,000 towards the recovery costs.

Today, old *R for Robert* is being preserved and restored at Brooklands Museum, Weybridge.

4

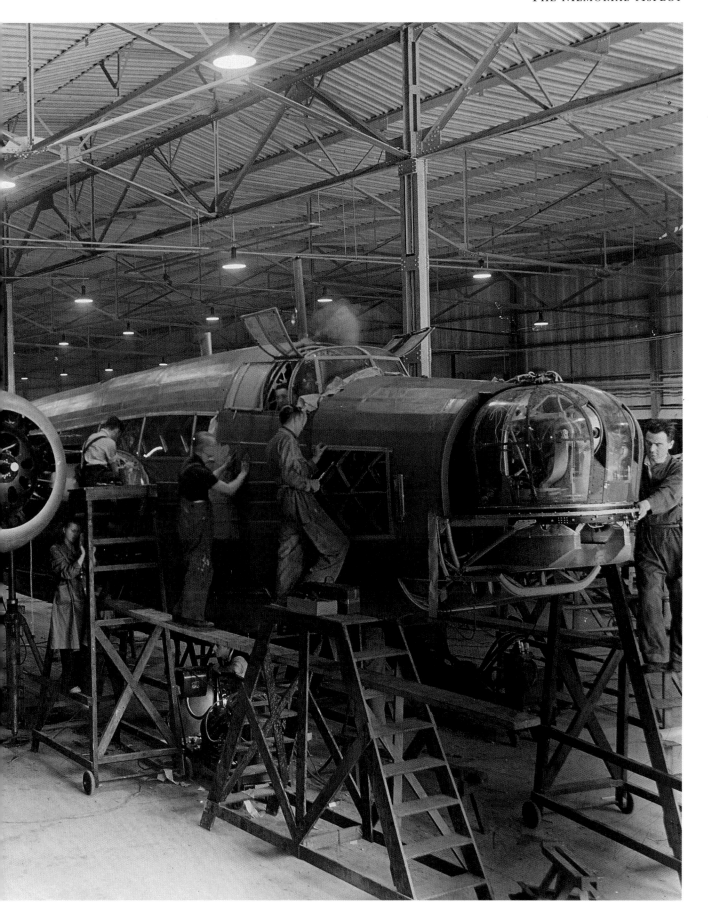

5. An aerial view of Wimpole in 1949 showing the South Avenue.

6 (detail)

6 (detail)

5   Wimpole Park, Cambridgeshire

The National Trust

Wimpole Park, near Cambridge, covers an area of 300 acres around one of the grandest eighteenth-century houses in Cambridgeshire, Wimpole Hall. The park is of outstanding importance as it retains examples of the work of Charles Bridgeman, 'Capability' Brown and Humphrey Repton, all of whom were important landscape gardeners of the eighteenth and nineteenth centuries.

The spectacular South Avenue, the creation in 1721 of Charles Bridgeman, who worked for Edward Harley, 2nd Earl of Oxford and owner of Wimpole at that time, is 2¼ miles long and was originally a double avenue of elms consisting of nearly a thousand trees. The Avenue was an immensely important local landmark for many decades: during the Second World War it helped to guide pilots in to nearby Bassingbourn and Bourn airfields. Part of the land between the double rows was concreted over and used for hard standing for military equipment. A temporary military hospital was set up in the park for the duration of the war.

In the late 1970s the Avenue was devastated by Dutch elm disease killing all the trees. So in 1980, NHMF provided a grant of £47,000 to enable the National Trust to begin the restoration of the Avenue. An appeal to raise funds for the reinstatement of the Avenue with limes sought sponsors for individual trees. Many contributors to the appeal used this opportunity to adopt trees for family and friends. Former members of the '91st', a United States squadron based at Bassingbourn during the war, have subscribed to two trees on the Avenue in memory of colleagues lost in action.

6   The Munitions Girls

STANHOPE FORBES RA

1918, oil on canvas, 101.5 × 127 cm
The Trustees of the Science Museum, London

During the First World War the iron and steel industry of South Yorkshire was almost totally turned over to the satisfaction of primary and secondary military needs. The call to the front had denuded the industry of skilled operatives, and women, who had left their traditional work, were now employed in machine shops and foundries, operating equipment which had formerly been the prerogative of men.

The Munitions Girls depicts the vitally important manufacture of 4.5-inch shells in the Kilnhurst Steel Works of John Baker & Co. It is a record of an industrial process, showing steel forging, in which billets are reheated in a separate furnace and, still glowing, manhandled to a steam hydraulic press for forging. Before the War this machinery had been used for the production of forged tyres and axles for railway wagons, but it had to be adapted to produce the overwhelming number of shells needed for the Western Front. The painting was commissioned in 1918 by George Baker, Managing Director of the firm, primarily as '. . . a memento for our women workers, and each of them received a framed copy of it'. The painting contrasts markedly in subject and treatment with Forbes's work as founder of the Newlyn School, but it retains the narrative content and social realism common in his paintings.

The Science Museum acquired the painting for £17,840, helped by a contribution of £13,380 from the NHMF.

7b

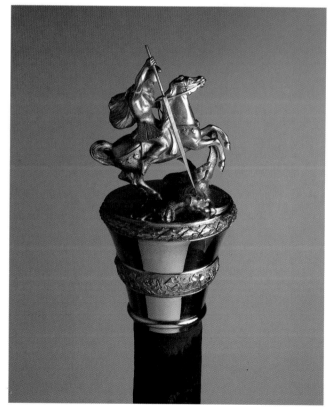

7g (detail)

7 *Collection of Orders, Decorations and Medals, and Field Marshal's Baton awarded between 1884 and 1920 to Field Marshal Sir John Denton Pinkstone French PC KP GCB OM GCVO KCMG, 1st Earl of Ypres (1852–1925)*

    a) Court-mounted group of fourteen medals
    b) Order of Merit, Military Division, Edward VII
    c) Prussia: Order of the Red Eagle, 2nd Class
    d) Austria: Order of the Iron Crown, Grand Cross
    e) Japan: Order of the Rising Sun with Paulownia Flowers, Grand Cordon
    f) Italy: Order of St Maurice and St Lazarus, Grand Cross
    g) Field Marshal's Baton
The Trustees of the Imperial War Museum, London

Sir John French's early career as a Cavalry Officer, first with the 8th (Queen's Royal Irish) Hussars and later with the 19th Hussars, was marked by considerable success. Before the First World War he held a number of increasingly important appointments, becoming a Lieutenant General and Inspector General of the Forces in 1907, and Chief of the Imperial General Staff in 1912. In April 1913 he received his Field Marshal's Baton.

With the outbreak of the hostilities in August 1914, French left for France as Commander-in-Chief, British Expeditionary Force, a position from which he resigned in December 1915 to be succeeded by Sir Douglas Haig. On his return to England French assumed the newly created appointment of Commander-in-Chief Home Forces. Created a Viscount in 1915, French became the 1st Earl of Ypres in 1922. In 1923 he was appointed Captain of Deal Castle and it was there that he died on 22 May 1925.

During his lifetime Sir John French received numerous honours both from his own country and from abroad. His collection of foreign orders includes examples from France, Belgium, Italy, Serbia, Japan, Russia, Romania, Austria and Spain, as well as from Imperial Germany. His British orders include the Order of the Bath, the Order of Merit, the Royal Victorian Order, and the Order of St Michael and St George, as well as his campaign medals for Egypt, the Sudan, South Africa and the First World War.

The collection of orders, decorations and medals, the Field Marshal's Baton and sixteen volumes of Sir John's diaries for the years 1900–1902, and August 1914 and July 1917 had been in the safe-keeping of the Imperial War Museum on loan for a number of years. In 1986 the Trustees were offered the opportunity of acquiring the complete collection on a permanent basis and sought the assistance of the NHMF to secure it for the nation. In January 1987 the collection was purchased for a total of £78,636, of which £68,636 was contributed by the NHMF.

8 *Papers of Field Marshal The Earl Haig (1861–1928)*

    a) Autograph diary from early August 1914 to 5 April 1919. Haig wrote every day in a series of pocket books

8b

on alternate (perforated) leaves, and regularly sent the upper copy to Lady Haig when he wrote home. This page shows the original diary entry for 11 November 1918, the day when the armistice came into effect.
    b) Copy telegram to Haig from the King
    c) Letter of congratulation from Ferdinand Foch (1851–1929), Marshal of France and Commander-in-Chief of the allied armies
    d) Photograph recording Foch's inspection of the guard of honour of the 6th Gordon Highlanders during his visit to Haig, 15 November 1918
The Trustees of the National Library of Scotland
ACC. 3155

In 1915 Field Marshal Haig commanded the 1st Army, but after Sir John French was recalled Haig was made Commander-in-Chief on the Western Front from 1915 until the end of the war. He was therefore responsible for the final victorious offensive in 1918, undertaken in co-operation with Marshal Foch. In 1918 Haig was granted an earldom, and in 1919 he was voted £100,000 by Parliament. He was instrumental in setting up the British Legion in 1921 and was its first president.

The letters, notebooks and papers of Field Marshal Haig, including the personal diary which he kept throughout the First World War, were deposited with the National Library of Scotland in 1961. When Lord Haig's family decided to sell the

8d

9. *Left medal.* Victoria Cross.

papers they were anxious that they should remain in Edinburgh and be purchased by the National Library. The Trustees of the National Library decided that they should make every effort to buy the papers, but recognised that in the face of potentially huge offers from overseas this would mean committing all the funds at their disposal and also having to appeal for help from other bodies. The National Library of Scotland purchased the papers in 1982 by private treaty for £450,000 with the help of a grant from the NHMF of £189,500.

9 *Warneford VC group*

Awarded June 1915
The Trustees of the Fleet Air Arm Museum
MED

Reginald Alexander John (Rex) Warneford was born in India in October 1891, the son of a railway engineer. He joined the Merchant Navy but transferred to the Royal Naval Air Service in 1915. Warneford learned to fly and gained a reputation as a born aviator, although a headstrong and somewhat reckless character. In May 1915 he joined No. 1 Squadron RNAS at Dunkirk. One of the squadron's tasks was to prevent Zeppelins attacking Britain from their bases in Belgium.

On the night of 6 June 1915 Warneford was one of a number of pilots trying to intercept two Zeppelins, LZ37 and LZ39, forced by bad weather to turn back from a raid on London. After a long chase Warneford managed to climb above LZ37 and drop his bombs on the Zeppelin beneath. The airship exploded in mid-air and threw Warneford's aeroplane across the sky. His engine stopped and he force-landed behind German lines. He eventually repaired a broken petrol pipe, and swung the propeller to start the engine, jumping into the cockpit of the moving aeroplane as a German patrol located him and opened fire, but they were just too late to prevent his escape.

LZ37 was the first Zeppelin destroyed by an allied aeroplane. The award of the Victoria Cross was prompted by King George V, and was notified to Warneford on 8 June, the first ever notification by telegram. It was only the second Victoria Cross awarded to an airman. Warneford was also made Chevalier de la Légion d'Honneur by the French authorities.

Only ten days after the award of the VC Warneford was killed while testing an aeroplane over Paris. His Légion d'Honneur medal, which he was wearing at the time of his death, was damaged as a result of the crash.

The medals remained with a branch of the Warneford family until 1987, when they announced their intention to sell them. The Fleet Air Arm Museum, determined that the medals should not go abroad, approached the NHMF for assistance. The group was purchased by private treaty for £55,000, and the NHMF provided £7,500. Further contributions included £20,000 from the MGC/V&A Purchase Grant Fund.

9. Flight Sub-Lieutenant Rex Warneford beside the aeroplane in which he shot down the Zeppelin LZ37.

10 *Manuscript drafts of* Memoirs of an Infantry Officer

SIEGFRIED SASSOON (1886–1967)

a) First complete draft of *Memoirs of an Infantry Officer*. It has as a frontispiece a pseudo-classical pen and ink drawing by his friend, the artist Rex Whistler

b) Subsequent draft of the work. It illustrates the extent to which Sassoon amended the manuscript at every stage of its composition.

The Trustees of the Imperial War Museum, London

The autobiographical works and war poems of Siegfried Sassoon have been recognised since their publication as among the most influential and outstanding personal testimonies of the First World War. *Memoirs of an Infantry Officer*, the second of a three-volume 'Life of George Sherston' (alias Sassoon), has amply justified predictions made of its lasting significance at the time of its publication in 1930. The book describes his experiences as a junior officer with the Royal Welch Fusiliers in the trenches on the Western Front in 1916 and 1917, and concludes with an account of his public protest against the continuation of the war when he was convalescing in England after being wounded in action.

These two notebooks in Sassoon's hand are from the series of heavily amended drafts that chart the progress of the book from his earliest jottings in November 1928 to the form in which it appeared in print two years later.

On the break-up of Sassoon's own library in 1975 the manuscripts were sold and acquired by an American bookseller. At that time, the Imperial War Museum was unable to make a realistic bid for the manuscripts, but in 1982, when they were offered for sale at Sotheby's New York, the generous assistance of the NHMF and the Dulverton Trust enabled them to be brought back to this country. The total cost of the purchase was £22,000, towards which the NHMF contributed £14,000.

11 *Evening in the City of London*

DAVID BOMBERG (1890–1957)

1944, oil on canvas. 69.8 × 90.8 cm
Signed and dated lower right
The Museum of London
85.219
EXHIBITIONS: *David Bomberg*, The Tate Gallery, London, 17 February–8 May 1988

This is the only painting Bomberg executed of London after the Blitz. The artist received permission to climb the tower of St Mary-le-Bow and the view he painted sweeps round from a gleam of the river on the south (left) over the familiar profile of St Paul's to Cheapside on the north (right). The gaunt outline of bombed-out London buildings provided Bomberg with a fitting subject matter to explore his fundamental concern with underlying forms, using the powerful medium of charcoal. However, in this work the drawing is enhanced by richly orchestrated textures to create a harmonious tonal scheme. It is an optimistic image, expressive of a firm intent to survive. As such it is among the most important icons created in London during the Second World War.

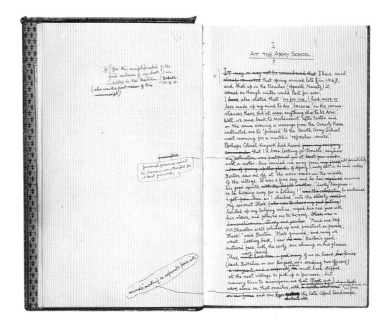

10b

10a. Rex Whistler's drawing.

11

Bomberg was the fifth child of Polish immigrant parents who moved from Birmingham to Whitechapel in 1895. He lived in Spitalfields until he left the Slade in 1913. His early work was influenced both by Cubism and Futurism, but after the First World War he turned away from machine-age imagery, developing a landscape style in Palestine and Spain during the 1920s and 1930s of increasingly expressive power and freedom. During the war he failed to achieve official recognition from the War Artists' Advisory Committee, and applied for over three hundred teaching posts without success. But he was given the task of recording an underground bomb store at Burton-on-Trent, and with the encouragement of his wife in 1943 he began a series of flower paintings and Welsh landscapes which renewed his interest in the possibilities of colour. When he returned to London, again acting as a fire-watcher, he began a series of bold charcoal drawings of the capital, in the hope that they would be published by John Rodker. The project fell through, but the drawings and this one painting remain.

The painting came up for sale in 1985. The assistance of the NHMF was needed because the total cost of £65,000 was greatly in excess of the Museum's purchase grant, even with substantial help from the MGC/V&A Purchase Grant Fund. The NHMF contributed £32,500.

12. Medals awarded to Lieutenant Robert Davies, *left* the George Cross.

12 *George Cross awarded to Lieutenant Robert Davies* RE

1940, St Paul's Cathedral, City of London
The Trustees of the Imperial War Museum, London

On the night of 12 September 1940 the City of London received one of its heaviest German bombing raids. Considerable destruction centred on the area round St Paul's Cathedral. Miraculously, the Cathedral itself was relatively unscathed. Daylight revealed, however, a large and deep hole in the pavement in Dean's Yard close to the West Front of St Paul's. A large unexploded device had penetrated the ground and travelled for some distance before coming to rest close to the Cathedral wall.

A Royal Engineers' Bomb Disposal Team, led by Lieutenant Robert Davies, was ordered in. After several hours of painstaking digging the Sappers found the bomb at a depth of some 20 feet close to burning gas mains and live electricity cables. They estimated it to be some 8 feet long and one ton in weight. Sapper George Cameron Wylie scraped away the clay, freeing the bomb, and then fitted the harness required to lift it clear and on to a waiting lorry. Davies himself drove the vehicle carrying the bomb along streets which had been specially cleared, to Hackney Marshes. The controlled explosion following detonation left a crater some 100 feet in diameter.

On 30 September 1940 the first awards of the newly instituted George Cross were announced in the *London Gazette*. Of the first three awards made two were to members of the Royal Engineers' team who had dealt with the bomb that had threatened St Paul's. One went to Sapper Wylie and the other, which subsequently became known as the 'St Paul's George Cross', to Lieutenant Davies.

It is believed that Davies sold his George Cross soon after the end of the War. For a number of years it seems to have been in the hands of a succession of private collectors, first appearing in auction in the early 1970s. In 1984 the Imperial War Museum bought the medal for £16,650, of which £10,650 was provided by the NHMF.

13 *Letter from Field Marshal Viscount Montgomery of Alamein (1887–1976) to General Sir Frank Simpson*

The Trustees of the Imperial War Museum, London

This is the first of an extremely important series of forty-nine letters which Field Marshal Montgomery wrote to General Simpson between October 1942 and September 1945. In it Montgomery, who had arrived in North Africa two months previously to take over command of the Eighth Army from General Ritchie, comments on the situation in the Western Desert shortly before the crucial Battle of El Alamein. He is particularly critical of the command structure which he had inherited and lists his own nominees for the key command positions under him. Montgomery had served with distinction as a divisional commander during the campaign in France in 1940, but it was his achievement in totally reversing the tide of the war in North Africa that won him public acclaim and established his reputation as Britain's foremost battlefield commander of this century.

Field Marshal Montgomery's professional relationship and personal friendship with General Simpson dated from their service together in the United Kingdom shortly before the Second World War, and the Field Marshal was later to describe Simpson as the best staff officer he had ever met. Montgomery's regular and detailed letters to Simpson, at that

12. Lieutenant Robert Davies in command of the Bomb Disposal Unit.

13. Lieutenant General Montgomery in command at the 2nd Battle of El Alamein, November 1942.

H.Q. 8ᵗʰ Army
M.E.F.
12-10-42

My dear Simbo,

I hope all goes well with you. I am enjoying life out here and have seldom felt better in my life. My first encounter with Rommell was of great interest; luckily I had had time to tidy up the mess (and it was "some" mess I can tell you) and to get my plans laid, so there was no difficulty in seeing him right off. I feel that I have won the first game, when it was his service. Next time it will be my service, the score being one-love. The situation here when I arrived was really unbelievable; I would never have thought it could have been so bad. Auchinleck should never be employed

13 (above and below)

again in any capacity; and I would never let Ritchie hold another command in the field: just at present (later on possibly). Good senior officers out here are scarce. I have already had out Harrocks, Leese, Krishman, Ankewright, Sugden; I tried to get Dudley Ward for the M.E. Staff College, but failed. I also tried to get you here as D.C.G.S., a Major-Generals job, but the War Office have said you cannot be spared. I think Steele is coming. I advised Alex to accept Steele when we knew we could not get you. You ought to come out here, and we will have another try later on. Write and tell me the news from home; one is rather cut off here. What have they done with Ritchie?

Yrs ever
B. L. Montgomery.

time Director of Military Operations at the War Office, provide a revealing chronicle of the campaigns that he conducted in North Africa, Sicily, Italy and north-west Europe. Although they were private letters containing many forthright expressions of his opinions, Montgomery always intended that Simpson should tacitly convey their contents to other senior officers in the War Office, since Montgomery had necessarily to be more circumspect in his official exchanges with Field Marshal Viscount Alanbrooke, the Chief of the Imperial General Staff.

Through the good offices of Sir Denis Hamilton, the Imperial War Museum purchased the letters by private treaty sale in 1983. Of the £22,000 paid for the collection, £18,000 was provided by the NHMF.

14 Holland I

Built by VICKERS, SONS AND MAXIM, 1901
Royal Navy Submarine Museum, Gosport

In 1982, following a faint clue in an old newspaper cutting, naval divers acting on behalf of the Submarine Museum discovered the intact wreck of the Royal Navy's very first submarine, HM Submarine Torpedo Boat No. 1, usually known as *Holland I* after her Irish-American inventor J.P. Holland. The little 'submarine boat', just 'the length of a cricket pitch' as the press described her in 1901 when she was built, was raised and immediately brought to Gosport from Devonport where she had been docked for initial conservation.

The submarine was in extraordinarily good condition. There was, inexplicably, very little internal corrosion even though she had been on the seabed for sixty-nine years after foundering under tow to the breaker's yard in 1913. *Holland I* is a unique example of the type of submarine adopted by most of the major navies at the beginning of the century. It was, in fact, fortunate that she sank in 1913, as otherwise nothing would be left to represent the realistic start of submarine services worldwide.

Despite help from Vickers who had built her 87 years ago, the Museum desperately needed money for the salvage and restoration. The NHMF came to the rescue with £19,000, about one-third of the cost of the project.

15 HMS Cavalier

'CA' Class Fleet Destroyer
built by J. SAMUEL WHITE AND CO. LIMITED, Cowes
laid down 28 February 1943
launched 7 April 1944
South Tyneside Metropolitan Borough Council

HMS *Cavalier* is the last surviving World War II destroyer of the Caesar Class. She was completed in November 1944 and joined the 6th Destroyer Flotilla, Home Fleet. In February 1945 she took part in three operations off Norway, 'Selenium', a strike against enemy shipping, 'Shred' to provide fighter cover for a minesweeping flotilla and 'Groundsheet', an aircraft minelaying strike. She was one of three destroyers sent from Scapa to re-inforce the escort of the

14

Arctic convoy RA 64, which had left the Kola Inlet on 17 February and been attacked by U-boats and enemy aircraft, and scattered during strong gales. After the war *Cavalier* was detached to the Western Approaches Command. She took part in many patrols and exercises until her long naval service finally ended in July 1972.

The HMS *Cavalier* Trust, anxious to preserve *Cavalier*, acquired her in 1977 and she was first open to the public as a Floating Museum dedicated to the Second World War destroyers at Southampton and later at Brighton Marina. In July 1987, she was acquired by South Tyneside Metropolitan Borough Council where she will be situated on the River Tyne which has long associations with Second World War destroyers.

In 1982 NHMF recognised the importance of HMS *Cavalier* and offered a grant of £25,000 to assure the preservation of the Destroyer as a public monument.

16 *Avro Lancaster Bomber*

The Trustees of the Imperial War Museum, London
(See colour illustration on p. 27)

The Avro Lancaster was the most numerous and successful of the British four-engined heavy bombers with which the Royal Air Force was equipped during the Second World War. Altogether 7,377 Lancasters were built, and by March 1945 there were no fewer than fifty-six squadrons of Lancasters in first-line service with Bomber Command. Lancaster bombers carried out 617 Squadron's famous 'Dam Busters' raid, led by Wing Commander Guy Gibson, as well as the attacks on targets such as the German battleship *Tirpitz*.

This particular example is a Lancaster B Mk X K B 889 built

15

in 1945 and is the only complete Lancaster of this period preserved in a public collection. The only other complete Lancaster in a public collection is in the RAF Museum at Hendon and represents a much earlier model.

The NHMF provided a grant of £130,000 which enabled the Imperial War Museum to purchase the disassembled Lancaster for restoration and eventual display at the historic RAF airfield at Duxford, in Cambridgeshire.

The Fund and the Church

CLAUDE BLAIR

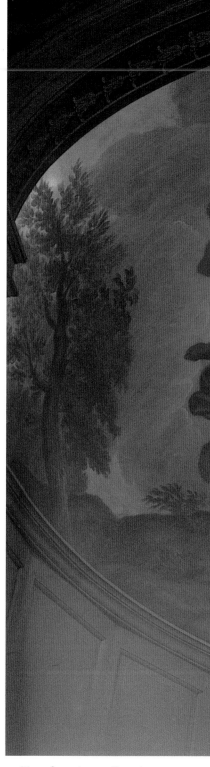

Probably something like 90 per cent of surviving English medieval art, excluding manuscripts and small archaeological finds, is in the custody of the Church of England, a body which is, of course, also responsible for a major section of the national heritage dating from later periods. Amongst these later holdings those of pre-nineteenth-century English figure-sculpture are of comparable importance to the medieval ones, since examples barely survive away from the funerary monuments with which our churches and churchyards are filled. The Church as a body has accepted responsibility, through the General Synod, for preserving all these works of art for the nation, but the conservation problems they present are horrendous, and it is ultimately the individual churches which own the objects that have to try and solve them. But the distribution of such objects is quite arbitrary and many of the most important belong to poor parishes – perhaps with fewer than twenty people on their electoral rolls – which may be struggling for their very existence. If such a parish is faced with the prospect of a major bill for conservation it will be eligible for various special grants, but the funds available to the bodies that make these is quite inadequate to meet all the demands, and, even if a grant is made, it is rare indeed for it to be for more than a proportion of the amount applied for. Where it is a question of conserving the fabric of an important historic church, a solution is, however, usually found: the parish, which clearly cannot continue to exist without a place for worship, either raises the money to put it in order, or the building is made redundant and vested in the Redundant Churches Fund for preservation as a national monument.

The question of the conservation of church fittings is more difficult. Not only is there not the same incentive to put them in order as there is for the building itself, but some incumbents and parish-councils question the propriety of diverting funds needed for carrying on the real work of the parish to what they regard, not unreasonably, as inessentials, or, in the case of family monuments, really someone else's responsibility. Also, all too frequently, parishes are faced with the task of conserving both their church and its fittings, and simply have not got the resources, however hard they try to raise money, to do both. It is here that the NHMF has given marvellous support as a last resort source of help when all others have been tried.

The NHMF seldom assists with the repair of the fabric of church buildings, but since its foundation it has given grants towards the conservation of fittings in one cathedral and more than a dozen churches and chapels, including the three represented in the exhibition (nos 17–19). Subjects of grants range from a modest painted royal coat of arms in Wickhamford Church, Worcestershire, to restoration work to the tower and spire of Sir George Gilbert Scott's great church of All Souls, Haley Hill, Halifax, as well as the bells of Durham Cathedral, the carved reredos of the chapel of Oxburgh Hall, Norfolk, two organs, and a number of monuments, both medieval and later. One of these last was the 6 ft. 4 in. oak effigy of a medieval knight which, having been stolen from Burghfield Church, Berkshire, was

17. *Transfiguration* attributed to Antonio Bellucci.

exported (without an export-licence!) to Belgium, where it was bought by a collector. Despite the fact that Burghfield had owned the effigy since the early fourteenth century, the parish, under Belgian law, was only able to recover it by purchasing it from the Belgian collector. It is a measure of the NHMF's good sense and flexibility that it gave a substantial grant for this purpose.

17

17. *Hope*, wall-painting in grisaille.

18c

17 *The church of St Lawrence (Whitchurch), Little Stanmore*

The church of St Lawrence was almost entirely rebuilt in 1715 by James Brydges, first Duke of Chandos, following his purchase of the Cannons estate in Little Stanmore. The Duke employed some of the most fashionable artists of his day to decorate his great mansion of Cannons, then under construction, and those same artists (Antonio Bellucci, Louis Laguerre, Francesco Sleter) created the strikingly dramatic interior of the church. The style is continental Baroque but with a touch of English restraint. The walls and ceiling are covered with paintings of biblical scenes, some in brilliant colours, others in subdued tones of sepia and grisaille. *Trompe-l'oeil* is used to considerable effect. The splendid woodwork includes columns and organ-case carved by Grinling Gibbons, and the organ keyboard on which George Frederic Handel would have played is still preserved. The Duke of Chandos was one of Handel's early patrons.

The condition of this unique church interior had begun to deteriorate rapidly in the 1960s: structural decay, flaking of plaster and efflorescence were causing problems, and major restoration was an urgent necessity. During the 1970s the north wall had to be demolished and totally rebuilt. That entailed the removal, cleaning and replacement of the murals, a lengthy and costly job. Between 1982 and 1985 the remaining ceiling and wall-paintings were repaired, cleaned and restored with infinite skill by a team of restorers from South

Germany. Their work was documented in a BBC 2 television programme, *Former Glory*.

The cost of a restoration programme of such size and complexity was far beyond the means of a small church congregation, however dedicated. Grants were sought from a variety of sources including, in 1981, the newly created NHMF. The NHMF responded promptly and generously with a grant of £15,000 and further grants in 1984 and 1985 brought the NHMF's total contribution to £29,978.

18 *St Nicholas, Stanford-on-Avon*

a) Figure of a female saint under a canopy *c.* 1325–1350, stained glass from the east window of the nave, south aisle, width 40 cm, height 168 cm
b) Eyelet fillings from the tracery showing birds and fish *c.* 1325–1350, stained glass from the east window of the nave, south aisle
c) Sir Thomas Cave (d. 1613) and his wife Eleanor St John with effigies of their five sons and three daughters. Early seventeenth century, alabaster

St Nicholas, Stanford-on-Avon, has been a place of worship for over nine hundred years. The present building was constructed in the first half of the fourteenth century, retaining the chancel of the Norman church but with enlarged windows; the nave, aisles and tower were completely rebuilt. Having been built over a relatively short period, the church has a unity in its interior and exterior which is unusual.

18a (detail)

The church contains one of the finest collections of fourteenth-century stained glass to be found in an English parish church. The main and tracery lights of the upper part of the east window date from the reign of Edward II. Much of the glass in the north side of the chancel, and in the east windows of both north and south aisles dates from 1325–1350 and includes an almost complete set of the twelve apostles and associated grisaille. There is also some very interesting sixteenth-century glass.

The monuments in St Nicholas are remarkable in that for a parish church they cover an unusually wide range of types and styles. The earliest monument is the effigy of Alan de Aslaghby, the priest who rebuilt the church, and who died in 1357. A series of eight monuments commemorating the Cave family associations with the church between 1558 and 1862 form one of the most remarkable groups of post-Reformation monuments in England. The church also contains a fine collection of seventeen hatchments to the Cave family.

The stained glass was in imminent danger of collapse and permanent loss, because of the deterioration of lead, ferramenta and stonework. In 1986 the NHMF offered a grant of up to £60,000 towards the restoration of this important stained glass.

The monuments are also suffering serious deterioration, mainly from rusting ferramenta. Several of the monuments have had to be completely dismantled and taken to a conservator for restoration. The NHMF is providing a grant of up to £72,500 towards this restoration.

19 *Sculptures from St Paul's, Jarrow*

Anglo-Saxon, *c.* 700, sandstone; bird panel: height 44.5 cm, width 29.2 cm; hunter scroll: height 29 cm, width 38.8 cm

Both of these Anglo-Saxon panels were found in St Paul's, Jarrow, which was dedicated in AD 685. The frieze depicting birds was discovered on the south side of the church when the school was built there in 1840 and built into the west face of the north porch of the church by Giles Gilbert Scott after his rebuilding of the nave in 1866. The hunter scroll is said to have been found in 1865 when the eighteenth-century nave of the church was demolished.

Despite the differing locations of discovery and the present differences in measurements, both pieces are carved in the same deep 'Roman' style and depict scrolls which are identical in detail. They plausibly therefore formed part of the same decorative scheme, although not necessarily in adjacent positions. It is possible that they may have decorated a secondary development in the church since their style is so closely linked with sculptures which must be later than the foundation date.

One piece depicts two well modelled birds pecking at a plant scroll. The top of the panel is truncated and the base plinth has been reworked. The plant is probably meant to signify the true vine, and the birds' creation, which is nourished by it, a theme common in other Northumbrian sculptures of the Anglo-Saxon period. The composition on the other panel is probably based on a Roman hunting scene, although its significance for the decoration of a Christian church is uncertain.

These panels are of outstanding importance not only because they represent some of the earliest decorative schemes in English churches, but also because they provide a stylistic link with the most distinctive early medieval monument of the British Isles, the high cross. The sculptures had suffered considerable damage and erosion from being in the porch. The NHMF offered a grant of £15,000 towards the removal of the sculptures, their conservation and redisplay in a controlled environment in the church.

19. Hunter Scroll

Archaeology and Treasure Trove

I.H. LONGWORTH

The task of preserving a meaningful sample of the past becomes ever more fraught. Nowhere is this more evident than in the field of portable antiquities, where the pace of discovery continues unabated. While much stems from the ordered world of controlled excavation, more still derives from chance discovery and from the activities of those who scour the land with metal detectors. For an age which seeks to gain a greater understanding of the past than the simple recovery of objects can provide, the increase in the use of metal detectors remains a particular source of concern. Not only are the circumstances of discovery rarely recorded in full, but increasingly the very findspot is not revealed or its true position is falsified.

In the case of gold and silver, some protection is offered by the laws of Treasure Trove but only if it can be demonstrated that the objects are likely to have been deposited with the intention of later recovery and that no one survives with a valid claim to ownership. If declared Treasure Trove then such objects pass to the Crown or to one of those bodies or individuals who retain rights through franchise. If declared promptly and in full, then the finder can expect a reward equal to the full market value of the object recovered. But though the Treasure Trove system has helped to preserve many spectacular items and hoards discovered in recent years the protection offered by the law is only partial. It cannot be applied to objects buried with the dead, nor can it be extended beyond gold or silver even though the objects concerned are often found in close association. Thus a pot containing a hoard of silver rings would be excluded along with any loose jewels which had not been set into the rings. Such associated objects, like all other antiquities taken from the soil, belong to the owner of the land in which they are found.

England is indeed fortunate that the vast majority of landowners are prepared to ensure the survival of these antiquities by presenting them to a national or local museum. In the case of those who wish to reap some financial gain from windfall discoveries or where Treasure Trove rewards need to be paid, money must be found to secure these treasures for the nation. Such calls are often unpredictable and many now lie beyond the resources of the museums concerned. It is here that funds like the NHMF have begun to play such a crucial role. As market prices continue to rise, many of the choicest and most important items which could so dramatically illuminate our remote past will be lost to the nation. Given present funding levels, purchase grants simply cannot keep pace. Already the NHMF has helped to save at least one major item from imminent export. Many more calls are likely to be made in the coming years.

20

but more importantly two painted reference numbers prefixed by the letters 'LC' (for Lowther Castle) and the vital painted inscription 'PENRITH CUMBERLAND' betray both the provenance and the origin of the sculpture.

In the late nineteenth century, Lord Lonsdale's sculpture galleries at Lowther Castle were justifiably famous. Amongst the classical splendours lurked at least three examples of pre-Norman English sculpture – two late eighth/early ninth-century cross-shafts from Lowther Churchyard, elaborately decorated with vine-scrolls and animals (and now in the British Museum and the Burrell Collection, Glasgow), and this crucifixion slipped out, unnoticed, in the 1947 sale of Lowther's contents as part of lot 2326 ('various fragments of sculpture, probably emanating from churches and other buildings in the vicinity and other unimportant fragments about 20'). After some years in private ownership, the crucifixion emerged on the London art market in 1981. It was eventually acquired by Abbot Hall Art Gallery for £3,800, with a grant of £950 from NHMF together with grants from the V & A Purchase Grant Fund and Kendal Town Council.

21 *The Achavrail Armlet*

First-second century AD, bronze, internal diameter
10 cm, height 6.2–9 cm
Inverness Museum and Art Gallery
INVMG. 987.050
EXHIBITIONS: *Origins of Design: Bronze Age and Celtic Masterworks*, Michael Ward, Inc., New York, October–December 1987

This massive bronze armlet, almost 800 g in weight, is a superb example of Celtic craftsmanship of the early 1st millennium AD. It is penannular in form, and cast with an external high-relief decoration of trumpet domes and keeled ribbons around the large circular terminals and along the triple bands. The interior is hollowed and its surface bears numerous tool marks, probably from the wax model stage of its production.

About twenty such Celtic armlets have survived the passage of time. They have almost all been found in eastern Scotland, with a concentration in Aberdeenshire, the supposed area of their manufacture.

The Achavrail armlet was found in 1901, while a field was being ploughed on the croft near Rogart in Sutherland. The crofter thought that he had found an old curtain ring until he took it to the Reverend Dr Joass, a minister and antiquarian of Golspie, who had established the archaeological collections at the Duke of Sutherland's museum at Dunrobin Castle. On realising the importance of his discovery, the crofter gave up the armlet to the Sutherland Estates. It remained on public display at Dunrobin until 1977 when the museum was forced to close owing to disrepair.

In 1986 the Achavrail armlet was offered for sale to the Royal Museum of Scotland, to raise funds for the renovation of Dunrobin Castle's museum building, collections and displays. However, the Royal Museum has a number of similar armlets in its collections and did not wish to add to them. Thus the armlet subsequently went to auction and, several months later, an export licence was applied for. Inverness District Council was determined to keep the armlet in

20 *Hiberno-Norse Plaque of the Crucifixion*
By unknown Hiberno-Norse artist-craftsmen working in the Penrith area of Cumbria in the tenth to eleventh century AD

Limestone, 30 × 32 × 6 cm
Abbot Hall Art Gallery, Kendal, Cumbria (normally on permanent display at Kendal Museum of Natural History and Archaeology)

This carved limestone depiction of the crucifixion was probably once a devotional wall plaque within the pre-Norman church at Penrith. It represents Christ, without a cross, with two attendant angels; the spearbearer, Longinus, pierces Christ's left side, whilst, to the right, the spongebearer, Stephaton, awkwardly holds a pole terminating in a trumpet-shaped cup or chalice. The heavily worn remains of a third attendant are visible beside Stephaton.

Originally the whole composition, once some 36 cm square, was brightly painted with polychrome pigments, traces of which – and of the underlying gesso – most unusually remain.

The iconography of this crucifixion isolates it from the hundreds of carvings which have survived from pre-Norman England and links it conclusively to Ireland, specifically to an openwork metalwork plaque from Clonmacnoise. Both depend on the same model-type circulating in Ireland, and the closely related areas of Man and western Scotland.

The reverse of the plaque is roughly punch-dressed, with an incised graffito of a boar, which is probably not original

Scotland, close to where this most northerly example was discovered. Its Common Good Fund purchased it for Inverness Museum and Art Gallery for the sum of £100,000, with a £14,500 grant from the NHMF and further financial aid from the NA-CF and the LMPF.

22 *Bronze Age Gold Torc from Sculthorpe, Norfolk*

1200–1000 BC, length 43.6 cm (max)
Norfolk Museums Service (Norwich Castle Museum)
253.986

This gold torc was found in 1984 on arable land by a farmer. It belongs to the Later Bronze Age 'four-flanged' type, made from a twisted bar of x-section, the ends capped with conical terminals. Originally it was circular with the terminals hooked round one another, but the shape has been distorted by farm machinery. The size suggests that it was worn round the waist, possibly as a symbol of rank rather than as a piece of jewellery.

Fourteen of these four-flanged and related Bronze Age gold torcs have been found in East Anglia. Although most such torcs are likely to have been made in Ireland, it has been suggested that there was a workshop in west Norfolk or east Cambridgeshire. Wherever it was made, this torc was obviously the work of a master craftsman.

21

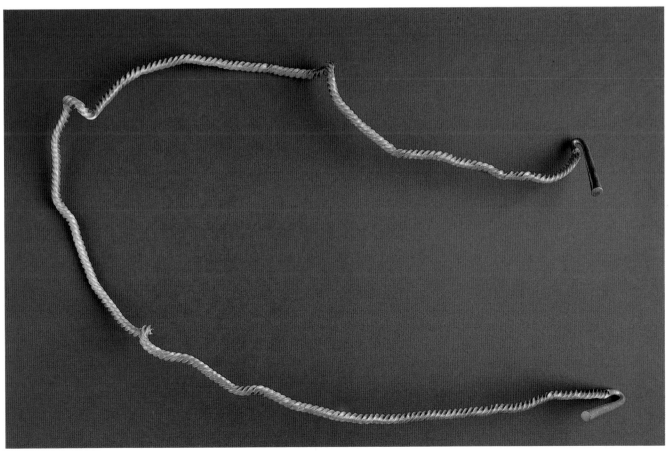

22

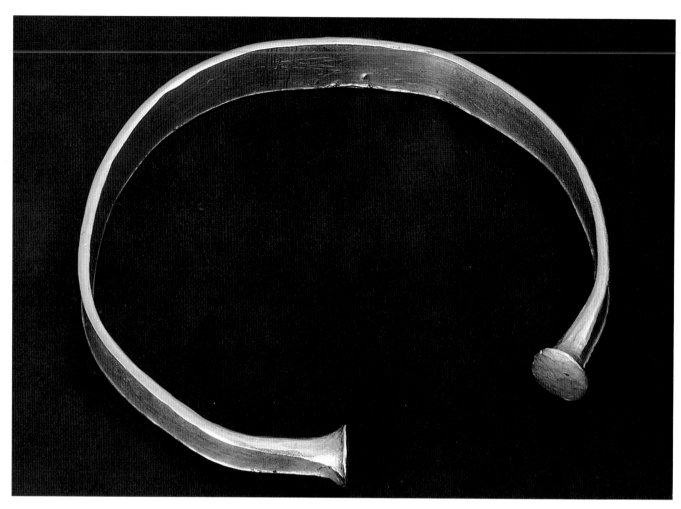

23

The torc was declared Treasure Trove in December 1985. The British Museum, who as representatives of The Crown may acquire items of Treasure Trove first, did not wish to purchase the torc. To acquire it, Norwich Castle Museum had to raise the £30,600 needed for the *ex gratia* reward paid to the finder. The NHMF provided £4,650 towards the total cost. The Museum also received grants from the MGC/V&A Purchase Grant Fund and the Pilgrim Trust.

23 *The Potterne Bracelet*

> Late Bronze Age, *c.* 900–750 BC, approximately 85 per cent gold, 12 per cent silver, 3 per cent copper, weight 25.54 g
> *Devizes Museum*
> 1983.75

This bracelet has a flat, ribbon-like body with a hammered edge. The ends revert to a rounded cross-section, with flattened circular terminals which resemble nail-heads. It is in excellent condition, showing very few signs of wear, the lipped edges still being sharp.

The bracelet belongs to a class of bracelets recognised only recently as such and found predominantly in south-west England and Wales. It has been called the 'Potterne type' of

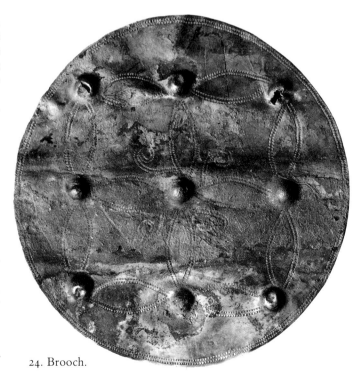

24. Brooch.

bracelet, and it was found by chance in 1982 at Potterne, near Devizes, in Wiltshire, on an archaeological site now known to have been inhabited from the late Middle Bronze Age to the Early Iron Age (approximately 1100 to 650 BC).

The particular importance of the bracelet lies in the place of its discovery. The findspot, because of its extent and richness as well as the fine preservation of the artefacts found on it, has been described as 'the most important later Bronze Age settlement site in the British Isles'. The finds from the exploratory excavations undertaken have been deposited in Devizes Museum, and it was crucial for the bracelet to join them. Devizes Museum houses the most important collection of Bronze Age antiquities in southern Britain, but being administered by an independent body, has to find support for major purchases.

The bracelet was purchased for £1,200 with the aid of a grant of £300 from the NHMF.

24 Disc Brooch and Coins from the Barsham Hoard

Late Saxon, c. AD 1000, silver,
diameter of brooch 11.3 cm
Ipswich Museums and Galleries
R. 1987-145

The brooch was found with sixty coins of Aethelred II. It consists of a thin disc, decorated on the front with a grid of nine small repoussé bosses and geometric and scroll decoration. The pin is missing, although there are traces of solder for its attachment on the back. This type of brooch came into fashion in the early ninth century, and continued to be made for about two hundred years. The closest parallel to the

Barsham brooch is a fragment from a Viking hoard dated to c. AD 1002, found at Sturkö, southern Sweden. It is likely that they were made in the same workshop.

The coins are all pennies in the name of Aethelred II (978–1016), of the Long Cross type, current c. 997–c. 1003. They were variously minted at London, Cambridge, Huntingdon, Thetford and Norwich. The hoard seems to have been deliberately buried for retrieval at a later date, c. 1002–c. 1003. Why it was not recovered will never be known, although it may have been hidden about the time that Swein Forkbeard, King of Denmark and father of the future King Canute, invaded East Anglia and sacked Norwich and Thetford. Sixty pence was a lot of money in late Saxon times, and in modern terms represents a sum of about £600.

The brooch was discovered folded into three and wrapped around the coins at a depth of about six inches on the south bank of the River Waveney at Barsham in Suffolk (TM 4035 9107), by Mr Remblance and his son. The brooch is important because it is so closely dated by the coins, and is one of the few pieces of late Saxon jewellery to have been found in Suffolk. The hoard was declared Treasure Trove, and valued at £9,160. The NHMF generously gave a grant of £6,600 towards its purchase.

25 The Freston Pendant

Anglo-Saxon, seventh century AD, gold, with garnet
centre, diameter 2.5 cm
Ipswich Museums and Galleries
R. 1987-142

This small circular gold pendant has a cabochon garnet centre and filigree decoration of beaded wires. The loop is unusual

24. A selection of the coins.

25

in being plain and not fluted. Similar pendants from Milton Regis and Wye/Crundale Down in Kent are dated to the seventh century.

The pendant was found by Russell Wright on the foreshore of the River Orwell at Freston, near Ipswich, on Saturday 10 August 1985 (TM 13NE 17993979). The findspot was a few inches below the surface. The object's condition shows little sign of contact with water or burial in the tidal zone, and, indeed, is in good condition.

It is unusual for a museum to have the opportunity to acquire such a high-quality piece of Saxon jewellery. Ipswich Museums already hold important Anglo-Saxon material, and considered it essential to make an all-out effort to purchase the pendant, thus keeping it in Suffolk available for everyone to see and study.

NHMF's grant of £1,000 was necessary to help secure the item through Christie's in 1986 with contributions also from NA-CF and the MGC/V&A Purchase Grant Fund. The total cost was £9,000.

26 Rudchester Roman Fort, Northumberland

Northumberland County Council

The Roman fort of Rudchester (Vindovala) is situated in Northumberland approximately 8 miles west of Newcastle upon Tyne. The fort was built at the time of Hadrian for a unit of five hundred troops some of whom were cavalry. The area enclosed by the ramparts of the fort is 4.5 acres and a civilian settlement (*vicus*) lies to the south-west. Hadrian's Wall joins the fort at the east and west gateways so that part of the fort lies to the north of the wall.

Earlier excavations in part of the fort have shown it to contain at least three periods of military buildings, and the fort having been abandoned some time after AD 370. The

limited excavations that have occurred at Rudchester indicate that there is potentially good survival of many buildings and other archaeological evidence relating to the history of this site in particular and the internationally famous Roman frontier in general.

The site was acquired by Northumberland County Council in 1983 with a grant of £30,000 from NHMF, enabling the Council to safeguard the site in the immediate future and to establish long-term strategies for the development and appreciation of Rudchester by a wider public.

27 Writing Tablets

c. AD 100, found at Roman fort of Vindolanda, near Hadrian's Wall, 1985; wood
The Trustees of the British Museum

a) Line from Virgil's *Aenead* (IX, 473) copied out as a writing exercise, 85/137, 10.0 × 1.5 cm

b) Military intelligence report, perhaps left by a commanding officer for his successor, about the fighting habits of the British (here disparagingly referred to as *Britunculi*, 'Little Brits'. It may be translated: '. . . the Britons are unprotected by armour(?). There are very many cavalry. The cavalry do not use swords nor do the wretched Britons take up fixed positions (or stay seated?) in order to throw javelins.' 85/32, 7.8 × 18.6 cm

c) Letter from Claudia Severa to Sulpicia Lepidina, wife of Flavius Cerealis, commander of a cohort of Batavians, who were stationed at Vindolanda from *c*. AD 100–105. Claudia Severa, who probably was the wife of the commander of another cohort stationed on Roman Britain's northern frontier, invites Lepidina to a birthday party. The letter may be translated:
'Claudia Severa to her Lepidina greetings.
On the 3rd day before the Ides of September, sister, for the day of the celebration of my birthday, I give you a warm invitation to make sure that you come to us, to make the day more enjoyable for me by your arrival, if you come.
Give my greetings to your Cerialis. My Aelius and my little son send their greetings. I shall expect you, sister. Farewell, sister, my dearest soul, as I hope to prosper, and hail.
To Sulpicia Lepidina (wife) of Flavius Cerialis; from Severa.' 85/57, 22.3 × 9.6 cm

These wooden tablets are three of about one hundred examples (in some 2,500 fragments) found at the Roman fort of Vindolanda, near Hadrian's Wall, in 1985. The tablets consist of thin leaves of wood with text generally written in ink. They comprise part of the oldest group of written documents known from Britain and consist mainly of letters, accounts and other material relating to the administration of the fort of Vindolanda at the end of the first century AD.

As the British Museum had purchased the wooden tablets previously found at Vindolanda, and had begun to develop a special storage system, it was desirable that the new discoveries should be added to the National Collections. In 1987 assistance was sought from the NHMF who generously granted £100,000 towards the total cost of purchase of £115,000.

26. Hadrian's Wall at Rapishaw Gap. Rudchester Fort straddles the wall to the east.

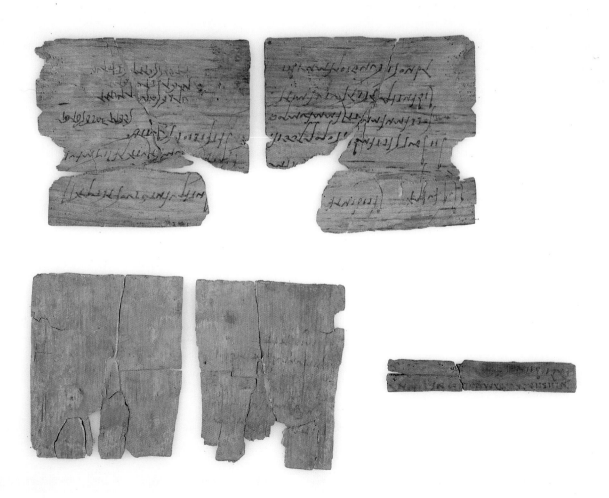

27. *Top:* c, *bottom left:* b, *bottom right:* a.

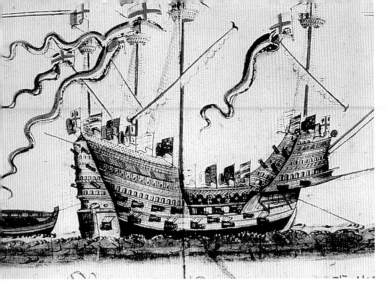

A contemporary illustration of the *Mary Rose* (*The Master and Fellows*, Magdalene College, Cambridge)

28 The Mary Rose, Portsmouth

The Mary Rose Trust

a) Icon, bone carving depicting two angels. Found within a chest on the main deck in the stern. Also in the chest was a leather pouch containing coins, dice, seals and a comb.

b) Bone manicure set, found in a personal chest on the main deck. Similar sets have been recorded at other Tudor sites including St Michael's House in Southampton.

c) Copper thimble and needles, from a collection comprising copper and bronze pins, wooden bobbins and thimbles, distributed throughout the ship and found mainly in association with personal chests.

d) Barber Surgeon's syringe, made from pewter and bronze and used to treat wounds, ulcers and venereal diseases.

e) Dividers, one of two pairs found inside a cabin on the main deck in the bow, beside a chest which contained the mariner's compass.

f) Piece of shot with shot mould, used for casting lead shot on board ship.

g) Pewter flagon bearing several scratched marks, including the date 1545 and another in the form of three fishes, reminiscent of the rebus adopted by the Salmon family. Robert Salmon Senior and Robert Salmon Junior were Masters of Trinity House in 1588 and 1617 respectively.

On a calm summer day in 1545 a French invasion fleet lay at anchor off Portsmouth, poised to attack England. On that day, Henry VIII's favourite ship *Mary Rose* sailed into her final battle. As the King watched from the shore, she heeled over and sank, taking with her seven hundred men. She had been built thirty-five years earlier, and had been named after the King's younger sister.

Efforts to locate the hull began in the mid-1960s. The Mary Rose Trust was formed in 1979 to undertake the complete excavation and recovery of the hull in a concentrated work programme. In 1982, after more than four centuries on the seabed, the hull of the *Mary Rose* was finally raised to the surface. The 17,000 objects recovered gave an intriguing insight into life on board a Tudor warship. Once removed from the seabed, both hull and objects needed immediate and vital conservation treatment to prevent any deterioration.

The NHMF played a crucial role in the Mary Rose Project, the world's most ambitious underwater archaeological project. Between 1980 and 1986 the NHMF contributed more than £1,200,000 in the form of loans and grants, making it the largest single source of British support for the project.

29 Collar of ss

c. 1440, silver, *c.* 61 cm
Museum of London

Collars of ss were the distinctive livery of the royal house of Lancaster and were granted by all three Lancastrian kings to those whom they wished to honour. It is thought that the ss stood either for *sovereyne* or for *souvenez*.

This silver collar is a chain of forty-one linked letters of s, meeting in an ornamental arrangement of buckles and links ending in a fluted ring. From this ring the owner might have hung a royal or family badge. The collar, which was recovered from the Thames foreshore in 1983, appears to date from the middle of Henry VI's reign, making it the only surviving collar of ss that can be regarded with certainty as medieval. Associated archaeological evidence and metallurgical analysis support this dating, while the best parallels for this type of collar appear on effigies of the 1440s and on the portrait (National Gallery, London) of Edward Grimston, painted by the Flemish artist Petrus Christus when Grimston was Henry VI's ambassador in Bruges in 1446.

One reason for the disappearance of medieval collars of ss was the deposition of Henry VI in 1461 and the accession of Edward IV and the Yorkist dynasty. Edward IV introduced his own livery collar of suns and roses, and it would have been imprudent for former supporters of the Lancastrian cause to have been found in possession of collars of ss. It is therefore possible that after the dynastic upheaval the owner of this collar disposed of it by throwing it into the River Thames.

The collar was adjudged by coroner's inquest not to be Treasure Trove and the Museum of London, with the agreement of other interested parties, acquired it after rewarding the finder, a licensed Thames mudlark, with the sum of £20,000, the collar's estimated market value. NHMF contributed £10,000 towards this amount and the Worshipful Company of Goldsmiths £5,000.

29

Museums and the Heritage

D.M. WILSON

A museum is not primarily a resource of entertainment nor of tourist revenue. It is not élitist and it is not expendable. A museum represents one of the higher products of human imagination in that it cares for man and his environment and for his products and his resources. It is an institution, to use an eighteenth-century term, for the 'curious' and its resources enrich the human condition and provide in a unique fashion for the heritage of mankind.

The primary functions of a museum are to collect, conserve and keep safe for the foreseeable future the objects committed to its care. At the same time there is an intellectual and spiritual content which cannot be denied. Museums should, therefore, be allowed the freedom to function for this purpose without inter-ference, political or moral. They rely for their collection on the taste and expertise and energy of their staff; they rely also on the public constituency which they serve and which has helped to form them. Accident and whim play a role in the formation of a museum, as existing collections are enriched by donation or purchase, as gaps are filled or as private people are forced to sell. But at base most museums have a coherent policy of acquisition.

Field-work based on carefully thought out acquisition policies brings to museums archaeological, ethnographic, artistic, natural-historical and geological material of prime importance. Gaps in a collection are also identified and filled by careful buying and by the encouragement of donations. New areas are selected for concentrated investigation. Often museums come late to the varying fields of collection, because they cannot easily form taste. It is usually the private collector who sets the pace. Thus, for example, Samuel Courtauld and Campbell Dodgson created the English taste for Impressionist and post-Impressionist painting and print-making, buying privately and with great discernment. Their collections, now in the National Gallery, the Courtauld Institute and the British Museum, stimulated further purchases by museums and galleries throughout the country. Museums do, however, also initiate collecting to build up the heritage. The British Museum, for example, has brought together very considerable collections, of more than curatorial importance, over many years, and most recently collections of German expressionist prints, modern medals and the only major working collection of banknotes in the public sector of the world. The Maritime Section of the National Museums on Merseyside has preserved not only material of import-ance to the history of the merchant navy, but also a major nineteenth-century security dock and the earliest surviving English dry dock.

The NHMF has generously funded an extraordinarily diverse range of objects for various museums in this country. Consider, for example, a pair of sixteenth-century silver-mounted tankards; Sir Donald Campbell's racing-car, Bluebird; a Rysbrack marble bust of the poet, Alexander Pope; the Doncaster Race Cup of 1845; the Peter Lazarus collection of English drinking glasses; early tanks for the Tank Museum at Bovington; a pair of Turner watercolours of Gibside in County Durham; the state bed of Queen Mary of Modena; and the Astor silver 'apostle' spoons. These are only some of the remarkable objects that have been purchased by museums with the aid of the NHMF – indeed, without the NHMF many of these great national treasures would have gone abroad, never to return.

30

Heterogeneous, almost perversely so, these items and the others acquired with the aid of NHMF add up to one of the greatest benefactions received by the nation's museums. By definition, most of this material is British and originates in British collections. Such acquisitions enrich not only existing collections but the nation.

As museums are encouraged by such generosity, so the private benefactor is also stimulated by it, giving to museums in emulation, but also in gratitude, objects which they have seen and enjoyed. For example, the British Museum for the tax years 1985 and 1986 received a total of 107 major donations and 832 minor donations (sometimes multiple gifts), and most public museums around the country will receive gifts on a commensurate scale. However diverse, these fit into collections and increase the whole.

Museums have had an image as dusty, dry, boring places. Even in the eighteenth century Ned Ward found the Ashmolean collections a 'warehouse of Antiquated Trumpery . . . Rusty Reliques and Philosophical Toys'. But such views today are clearly wrong, or museums would not be visited to the extent they are. The major national museums in London, for example, welcomed 22 million visitors in 1986. Nowadays museums are vibrant, exciting places – yearly improving their displays, increasing their scholarship and adding to knowledge – a worthy jewel in the cultural crown of any country.

The first illustrated book on the collections of the British Museum was published in 1778 by John and Andrew van Rymsdyk. Its opening words provide a view of preserved heritage which is as true today as it was then:

> Every rational Being should, nay, is obliged to bequeath something to Posterity, that it may be known that there was once such a person who intended to prevent the destruction of *Human Knowledge*, from the Sithe of Time; and to *Eternize* the Memory, or *Actions* of all such Men as have signalized themselves in Merit. These various Productions, or *Legacies*, are generally entitled the *Last Will and Testament* amongst *Painters*, or *Authors*, and have in all polite Nations been carefully preserved in Repositories or such a noble Cabinet as the BRITISH MUSEUM.

The NHMF and many other donors to public museums could well be satisfied with such a description of the motives behind their gifts. Through their generosity the heritage of the human mind is enriched.

31

30   The Concert

HENDRICK TER BRUGGHEN (1588?–1629)

c. 1626, oil on canvas, 99.1 × 116.8 cm
The Trustees of the National Gallery, London
6483

In this painting, which has strong claims to be Hendrick ter Brugghen's finest treatment of a secular subject, the artist has taken a scene favoured by Caravaggio and his Roman followers, a group of flamboyantly dressed musicians seen by candlelight, and treated it in his own distinctive manner, placing the dramatically lit half-length figures against a light background.

Ter Brugghen trained in Utrecht and spent almost a decade in Rome before returning to Utrecht in 1615. Along with a group of other talented artists from Utrecht who visited Italy at this time, he was greatly influenced by the work of Caravaggio and his immediate followers. This group is known as the Utrecht Caravaggisti. The large-scale half-length figures, their crowding together within the composition and their closeness to the edge of the canvas and the bright, colourful palette are all features which can be found in paintings by Caravaggio and his followers, such as in Caravaggio's *Musical Party* (Metropolitan Museum of Art, (New York)). Ter Brugghen brings to this existing format an individual fluency in modelling the soft edges of his forms and a remarkable subtlety of palette, which includes light blues, lemon, purple and cerise.

The painting was in the Somers collection at Eastnor

Castle, Herefordshire by about 1700. There are apparently no early inventories of the collection but the seventeenth-century Dutch paintings are said to have been purchased by Lord Somers, William III's Lord Chancellor. He made numerous trips to The Netherlands around 1700 and presumably bought his Dutch paintings there. The picture passed by descent to The Hon. Mrs E. Hervey-Bathurst, who in 1982 sold the painting to a consortium of art dealers from whom it was purchased for £1.725 m by the National Gallery in May 1983 with the aid of a grant of £500,000 from NHMF, and donations from the Pilgrim Trust and the NA-CF.

31   The Opening of Waterloo Bridge ('Whitehall Stairs, June 18th, 1817')

JOHN CONSTABLE (1776–1837)

Exhibited 1832, oil on canvas, 130.8 × 218 cm
The Trustees of the Tate Gallery, London
T 04904

This magnificent example of Constable's late style depicts the opening of John Rennie's Waterloo Bridge on the second anniversary in 1817 of the Battle of Waterloo. At the left the Prince Regent, later George IV, is shown about to board a royal barge at the landing of Whitehall Stairs. Numerous vessels, including the Lord Mayor's barge at the right, prepare to accompany him on his way to open the new bridge, seen in the distance with St Paul's behind it.

Over a period of about thirteen years Constable made

numerous drawings and oil sketches for a painting of the subject but only completed this definitive version in 1832. Although praised by many observers at the time, the painting remained unsold during Constable's lifetime and was knocked down at £63 in his studio sale in 1838. It subsequently changed hands several times before being acquired by Sir Henry Tennant in 1892. From him it passed to Lord Glenconner and in 1955 to the father of the anonymous owner who offered it for private treaty sale to the Tate Gallery in 1987. The asking price of £4 m was reduced to just under £3 m through tax concessions but this figure was still way beyond the Tate Gallery's means. The NHMF made a grant of £1.5 m towards the purchase price of just under £3 m. With additional grants from the Clore Foundation, the NA-CF, the Friends of the Tate Gallery and donations from many other organisations and individuals, the Gallery was at last able to secure this masterpiece for the nation.

32 *Gimcrack with John Pratt up on Newmarket Heath*

GEORGE STUBBS (1724–1806)

c. 1765, oil on canvas, 100.3 × 127 cm
The Syndics of the Fitzwilliam Museum, Cambridge
PD. 7-1982
EXHIBITIONS: Tate Gallery, 1982, as part of the campaign to save the painting for the nation; *George Stubbs 1724–1806*, Tate Gallery and Yale Center for British Art, 1984–5, no. 56

Gimcrack was one of the most famous racehorses in England in the eighteenth century. Foaled in 1760, his name lives on in the Gimcrack Stakes and the Gimcrack Club, as well as in the Gimcrack Club in New York. At just over fourteen hands he was an unusually small colt; but what he lacked in stature he made up in spirit, winning twenty-eight of his thirty-six races in a career which spanned eleven years.

In April 1765 he made his début at Newmarket, where he won his first race carrying the colours of William Wildman, a Smithfield meat salesman. This painting may have been commissioned to celebrate this victory, although a mezzotint by Pether published in May 1766 records that the jockey is John Pratt, riding groom to Viscount Bolingbroke, Gimcrack's second owner.

In all, Stubbs painted three compositions of Gimcrack, of which this is the most daring. The expanse of sky and characteristic flatness of Newmarket Heath act as a foil to the exquisitely painted figures of horse and rider, poised in a moment of pre-race tension: one of the rubbing-down houses behind them, the chances of the race to come. Stubbs here combines an intimate knowledge of equine anatomy with an extreme sensitivity to the landscape to make this one of the greatest masterpieces of British sporting art.

In 1957, the painting was acquired by Lady Adeane, on whose behalf it was almost immediately offered as a loan to the Fitzwilliam Museum. In 1982 the painting was put up for sale. The application for a licence to export to New York being withheld, the Museum had but four months to find £601,057. In recognition of its superb quality and quintessential Englishness the response of the NHMF of £229,000 was

32

immediate and generous. A public appeal led by contributions from Their Majesties The Queen and Queen Elizabeth, The Queen Mother, the Government Fund for the Regions, the NA-CF, the Pilgrim Trust and the British Sporting Art Trust helped ensure that 'the sweetest little horse that ever was' found a permanent home at Cambridge, only a few miles from the scene of his greatest triumphs.

33 *Mr and Mrs Coltman*

JOSEPH WRIGHT OF DERBY (1734–97)

c. 1770–2, oil on canvas, 127 × 101.6 cm
The Trustees of the National Gallery, London
No. 6496
EXHIBITIONS: *Acquisition in Focus*, National Gallery, London, 1986

In Joseph Wright's Account Book this painting is listed among the entries for 1770–71 as 'Mr & Mrs Coltman a conversation, £63'. Thomas Coltman (1746–1826) was a friend of Wright's, resident in Derby and at Gate Burton House in north Lincolnshire (the house in the painting), although in 1768 he had inherited the family estate of Hagnaby Priory also in Lincolnshire. He is shown with his first wife, Mary Barlow, whom he married in 1769 and who died in 1786.

In his monograph on the artist (1968), Benedict Nicolson describes the painting as an 'undoubted masterpiece'. Here, for the first time in Wright's art, are combined sensitive portraiture, lively animal painting, a convincing landscape setting, the genre quality of the conversation piece, and the naturalistic lighting effects for which he was so celebrated in his lifetime. The effect is at once both strikingly novel and deceptively unstudied.

Joseph Wright is best known for his candlelight pictures and for his depiction of contemporary scenes of industrial and scientific interest. However, the greater part of his work consists of portraits and he also painted landscapes and subject pictures. He was born at Derby, and trained in London under Thomas Hudson and John Hamilton Mortimer. On returning to Derby he established himself as a portrait painter. He

33

visited Italy from 1773 to 1775 and then spent two years in Bath before taking up residence again in Derby, where he remained until his death.

Like George Stubbs, Wright aimed for a scientific truthfulness of observation in his paintings, and his representation of the horses in this picture was almost certainly influenced by Stubbs. The pose of Thomas Coltman may derive from the figure of John Milbanke in *The Milbanke and Melbourne Families* in the National Gallery, which Stubbs painted a few years earlier, and it might well have been Stubbs' example that led Wright to adopt the less than life-size, full-length portrait format, which is relatively rare in his work.

The painting remained in the sitters' family until it was sent to auction at Christie's in 1984. It was purchased by the National Gallery for £1,419,600, towards which the NHMF contributed £400,000 and the Pilgrim Trust £20,000.

34 *Writing Cabinet*

JOHN CHANNON (1711–*c*.1783)

London, *c*. 1745–50, mahogany, with gilt-brass mounts and inlay, height 245 cm, width 117 cm, depth 76 cm
Leeds City Art Galleries
23/85

Of serpentine design, the lower stage of this writing cabinet has four long drawers; the top one, which pulls out on divided corner trusses, is fitted for writing. The upper part is unusual in being fronted by double doors which open to form deep wings incorporating tiers of folio divisions, pigeon holes and shallow drawers; the body contains a similar arrangement of storage units but centres on a door enclosing a complicated system of sliding panels, released by spring catches, which conceal seventeen secret compartments. The exterior of the cabinet is lavishly styled with engraved brass inlay and flamboyant mounts in Rococo taste while the cornice is headed by brass statuettes freely derived from the Venus de Medici and the Faun in Rosso Antico.

John Channon, cabinet-maker of St Martin's Lane, signed a spectacular pair of bookcases at Powderham Castle, near Exeter, embellished with engraved brass inlay and dated 1740. This was an unusual decorative technique at the time and, on the evidence of stylistic analogy, a group of high-quality cabinet furniture (much of it rather Germanic looking) exhibiting the same distinctive characteristics and technical features has been attributed to Channon's workshop. This writing cabinet is generally regarded as his finest achievement and one of the greatest pieces of English furniture.

The cabinet passed by descent to Sir William P.K. Murray of Ochtertyre, Perthshire, Scotland, before being sold at Christie's (30 June 1949, lot 130) to Major Arthur Bull. In 1985 it was most generously offered by the beneficiaries of his estate to Leeds as a private treaty sale and purchased for £211,000 with the aid of a grant of £70,000 from the NHMF. Had it been placed on the open market there is every likelihood that this celebrated cabinet would have left these shores forever.

34

34 (detail)

35

35   The Rutland Psalter

c. 1260, bodycolour on vellum, 28.5 × 20 cm
The British Library
Additional MS 62925

The Rutland Psalter is one of the greatest masterpieces of thirteenth-century English painting. It is not known for whom the book was originally intended nor exactly where it was made, but there can be no doubt that the first owner was a person of great consequence. Recent opinion suggests London as the most likely source and there seems to be some connection with the De Lacy family. The obit of Edmund de Lacy, Earl of Lincoln, who died in 1258, has been added to the calendar by a contemporary hand. In the fifteenth century the manuscript came into the hands of John Clifton, a prior of Reading Abbey, who gave it to his monastery.

The Psalter contains six large miniatures, nine historiated initials and a wide variety of lesser decoration including a sequence of calendar illustrations. It is particularly important for its marginal ornament, which includes scenes from everyday life, animals, monsters, grotesques and mythological subjects. This type of decoration was to become very fashionable on both sides of the Channel by the end of the thirteenth century but the Rutland Psalter provides the first major example in an English context. At least four artists participated in the making of the book.

Although the outstanding importance of this manuscript

35 (details)

has been recognised since the end of the nineteenth century, recent scholars have been obliged to rely on a monochrome facsimile published in 1937 for their knowledge of it. The Psalter was purchased by the British Library in November 1983 through a private treaty sale which conferred substantial benefits on vendor and purchaser alike. The NHMF provided £400,000 towards the purchase price.

36 *The Virgin and Child with Angels*
JOOS VAN CLEVE (fl. 1511–*c*.1540)

c. 1520–25, oil on oak panel, 85.5 × 65.5 cm
Trustees of the National Museums and Galleries on Merseyside
(Walker Art Gallery, Liverpool)
WAG 9864

Cleve-born Joos was one of Antwerp's leading artists, elected dean of its artists' guild several times before his departure for France at the request of Francis I. This excellently preserved central panel of a triptych displays the precise observation and sparkling colour characteristic of the early Netherlandish School's best productions. The Virgin and sleeping child are shown seated under a canopy attended by a choir of wingless Leonardesque angels, one of whom bears a bowl of cherries. The fruit and the marvellous naturalistic still life in front of the holy couple contain the predominantly eucharistic symbolism relating to Christ's Passion. The subtle nuances of light and texture are evident in every detail from the unusually patterned cloth beneath the Virgin's feet to the minute figure of a woman laying out laundry in the landscape at the right.

This relatively early work hung at Ince Blundell Hall, near Liverpool, from the date of its purchase by Charles Blundell in about 1835 until 1961, as part of a prestigious collection of Old Master paintings and antique marbles (the latter now in Liverpool Museum). The Blundell family did much to encourage local talent and patronage of the arts in Liverpool. The painting passed by descent to Colonel Sir Joseph Weld, and was purchased by private treaty sale in 1981 from the Trustees of the Weld heirlooms settlement with the help of £31,250 provided by the NHMF. It was the most important and relevant addition for many years to the Walker Art Gallery's collection of early Northern paintings which includes works by Cranach, Jan Mostaert and the Master of the Virgo inter Virgines, many acquired by Blundell's contemporary, the celebrated connoisseur, William Roscoe, with whom he shared a taste for early Northern and Italian pictures.

37 *Deposition of Christ*
JACOPO ROBUSTI called TINTORETTO (1518–94)

1550s, oil on canvas, 164 × 127.5 cm
National Galleries of Scotland
2419

The *Deposition of Christ* was executed in the 1550s having been commissioned by the Bassi brothers for their chapel in San Francesco della Vigna in Venice, which was conceded to the family in 1548. Nicknamed after his father's trade of dyer

36. Illustrated in colour on p. 14.

(*tintore*), Tintoretto worked almost exclusively in Venice, aiming, according to Raffaello Borghini, a contemporaneous Florentine writer, at a synthesis of Titian's colour and Michelangelo's draughtsmanship. The scene shown is described in St John's Gospel. Joseph of Arimathea (with a white beard) assisted by Nicodemus (in the striped robe) takes Christ's body to the tomb. The Virgin Mary swoons in the foreground attended by Mary Magdalene and Mary, mother of James.

The painting was once arched and framed by the altar's architectural surround. Its original format was recorded by Vasari in 1568, and is portrayed in early engravings with an upper section, now lost, showing an angel holding a crown of thorns. Restoration in 1984 revealed the angel's feet at the top of the canvas.

The painting was probably damaged when it was stolen from the church at some time between 1603 and 1631. It re-emerged in the collection of Louis, Duc d'Orleans, in 1727, having apparently been purchased from Madrid. It was sold at the Lyceum sale in London in 1798 to the 3rd Duke of Bridgewater and passed by descent to the present Duke of Sutherland. In 1984 the National Galleries of Scotland purchased the picture by private treaty, along with three other paintings from the Ellesmere Trustees, for the combined sum of £2 m. This was only made possible by a grant of over £1 m from the NHMF. The Fund's generosity enabled the *Deposition* to remain in the Gallery where it had been on loan since 1946.

37

38 *Landscape with the Ashes of Phocion*

NICOLAS POUSSIN (1593/4–1665)

1648, oil on canvas, 116.5 × 178.5 cm
Trustees of the National Museums and Galleries on Merseyside
(Walker Art Gallery, Liverpool)
WAG 10350

This masterly landscape was painted, with its companion *Landscape with the body of Phocion carried out of Athens* (on loan to the National Museum of Wales), in 1648 for the wealthy Lyons silk merchant, M. Cerisier, a close friend of the artist. It is one of a few paintings created by Poussin, the progenitor of French classicism, which raised the then subordinate genre of landscape to the status of figure painting. The *Phocion* paintings were the prototypal 'heroic' landscapes.

According to Plutarch, the Athenian general Phocion (402–317 BC) was a model of incorruptible civic virtue, whose support for the oligarchical party incurred the people's hatred and led to his being falsely accused of treason, sentenced to death and his cremation within Athens forbidden. Phocion's widow had to gather his ashes clandestinely from the Megara-Attica border, returning home with them for a public burial once the political climate changed. Within this ordered landscape the tension of her actions is heightened by her companion turning as if looking out for danger, perhaps sensing the crouching youth observing them from the nearby grove. Poussin was attracted to the tale's stoic theme of unjust

treatment and posthumous recognition of the 'honest man', and from it developed his grandest and most elevating conception of nature, a fact acknowledged by his contemporaries. It was of this painting that Bernini commented, whilst indicating his forehead, 'Poussin is a painter who works from here'.

After its purchase in about 1776–7 by the 12th Earl of Derby, the painting hung at the family's Liverpool seat of Knowsley Hall, Prescot, until it was offered for sale by private treaty in 1983. Because of the family's longstanding historic ties with the area the vendors were keen for the picture to stay on Merseyside. After nationwide publicity, one of the country's most important landscapes by Poussin was purchased by the Walker Art Gallery with the help of a grant of £706,210 from the NHMF.

39 *Shakespeare*

JOHN MICHAEL RYSBRACK (1694–1770)

1760, marble
Birmingham Museums and Art Gallery

Rysbrack's bust of Shakespeare is life-size and shows the playwright in early seventeenth-century dress. The marble is finely carved with a delicate detailing to the costume and to the head. The folds of the cloak are handled in a restrained

39

40

baroque style. The personality portrayed is serious, even noble, with emphasis on the bone structure of the head. The hair, moustache and beard are given an aristocratic elegance not found in the near contemporaneous portraits of Shakespeare that Rysbrack is known to have studied. The bust is hollowed out at the back and inscribed 'Mich¹: Rysbrack. Sculp^t:/ 1760'.

George Vertue records Rysbrack coming to England from Antwerp in 1720 and almost immediately being taken up by the architect James Gibbs. Rysbrack then dominated the sculptural scene for two decades producing portrait busts of historical figures as well as contemporaries, statues for monuments, and relief sculpture for architectural settings. Roubiliac became a significant rival from 1738 and Peter Scheemakers from 1741. Rysbrack continued, however, to enjoy major patronage into the 1760s, for example at Blenheim and Stourhead.

Rysbrack's first *Shakespeare* (1732) was among a group of historical busts made for the Temple of the British Worthies at Stowe. When, twenty-five years later, James West, a leading antiquarian and collector, commissioned a marble *Shakespeare* for Alscot Park near Stratford-upon-Avon, he chose the leading exponent of historical portraiture and supplied him with the best available evidence for Shakespeare's physical appearance, a cast from the monument at Stratford recognised as comparable to the folio engraving, both of the 1620s. Rysbrack also studied a copy of the Chandos portrait, which he declared had no 'spirit in it'.

The bust remained at Alscot Park from 1763 until 1986. Following sale at Christie's an export licence was suspended

which enabled the Birmingham City Art Gallery to raise the necessary £308,000. This was achieved through grants from the City, the NA-CF, Mr J. Paul Getty Jr and £150,000 from the NHMF. Without the substantial support of the NHMF Rysbrack's bust of Shakespeare would have been exported.

40 *Alexander Pope*

JOHN MICHAEL RYSBRACK (1694–1770)

1730, marble bust on black marble base, height 68.3 cm
National Portrait Gallery, London
5854

This noble portrait of the great Augustan poet, Alexander Pope, is one of Rysbrack's most accomplished works. It is a penetrating characterisation which conveys a remarkable spiritual intensity. Horace Walpole thought it 'very like', and this is confirmed by Pope's own dislike of it. He is reported by a contemporary as having 'ordered several Pictures and Busts of himself, in which he would have been represented as a Comely Person; but Mr Rysbrack, scorning to prostitute his Art, made a Bust so like him that Pope returned it without paying for it'.

Sir Joshua Reynolds, who never forgot the moment when, as a youth, he shook the great poet's hand, described him as 'about four feet six high; very humpbacked and deformed . . . he had a large and very fine eye, and a long handsome nose . . . an extraordinary face'.

It is likely that the bust belonged to James Gibbs, the

architect of Pope's Thames-side villa at Twickenham. The bust is an early work of the Flemish-born sculptor, Rysbrack, who owed his initial success in England to the many commissions for church monuments which Gibbs contracted to him. It probably passed with James Gibbs's estate to the Scottish painter, Cosmo Alexander. Later it was given by Sir William Garrow to Edward Badeley and is first certainly mentioned in 1868 in Badeley's will when it was bequeathed to the Athenaeum Club. The Athenaeum offered the bust for sale at Christie's in December 1985 but, following public outcry, it was withdrawn and offered to the National Portrait Gallery as a private treaty sale. The price of £395,000 was far beyond the Gallery's reach but in view of the bust's outstanding importance, the total amount was most generously provided by the NHMF.

41   *The Enchanted Castle*

CLAUDE GELLÉE (CLAUDE LORRAIN) (1600–82)

1664, oil on canvas, 88.5 × 152.7 cm
The Trustees of the National Gallery, London
No. 6471
EXHIBITIONS: *Acquisition in Focus*, National Gallery, London, 1982; *Claude Lorrain (1600–1682)*, National Gallery of Art, Washington DC, 1982

Claude Gellée, called from his birthplace Claude Lorrain by the French and celebrated by the English as Claude, was the most esteemed landscape painter in seventeenth-century Europe. Born in 1600, he left Lorraine at the age of thirteen for Italy, settling in Rome and specialising in landscape. By the 1630s he was well established, patronised by the King of Spain and the Roman aristocracy. For fifty years his explorations of light and space were sought by collectors throughout Europe.

In 1664 and 1665 Claude painted two subjects from the story of Psyche for Onofrio Colonna, Constable of Naples and one of his most important patrons: the first was the present painting, described in the seventeenth century as 'Psyche on the seashore' and much admired; the second, *Psyche saved from drowning*, is now in the Wallraf-Richartz Museum, Cologne.

The story of Psyche's love for Cupid, told by Apuleius, is one of successive abandonment and disappointment, until at last her fidelity is rewarded, she is turned into a god and the couple are allowed to marry. Psyche is shown near the sea, pensive in front of Cupid's castle 'built by no human hands, but by the cunning of a god'. But which episode in the story is represented here? Critics have suggested that it may show Psyche abandoned by her sisters (who can perhaps be seen in the small boat) after they have urged her to find out the identity of her mysterious lover; that it is the slow moment of delicious but fearful anticipation as Psyche prepares to enter Cupid's castle, where her unknown lover will come to her; or that she has already incurred Cupid's anger by lighting the lamp and discovering who he is and has now been left despondent, unable to follow him in his winged flight.

Such a range of response is proof, if proof were needed, of the picture's continuing power to intrigue. In early

41

41 (detail)

nineteenth-century England it became almost an icon of the romantic imagination. We know that it fascinated Hazlitt with its 'one simple figure in the foreground, "sole sitting by the shores of old romance"'. And on 25 March 1818 Keats wrote a verse letter on the painting (or on an engraving after it) to his friend John Hamilton Reynolds:

> You know the Enchanted Castle it doth stand
> Upon a Rock on the Boarder of a Lake . . .

A recollection of the painting may well be the inspiration behind the familiar lines in the 'Ode to a Nightingale':

> Charm'd magic casements, opening on the foam
> Of perilous seas, in faery lands forlorn.

The picture was in England, with its pendant, by the 1770s. In 1974, the painting was put on long loan to the National Gallery from the Loyd Collection. In 1981 it was offered for private treaty sale. The purchase of such a celebrated picture would have placed great strain on the National Gallery's limited resources: generous grants of £500,000 from the NHMF and £50,000 from the NA-CF allowed the Gallery to acquire the picture for the nation.

42 *Chestnuts*

SIR STANLEY SPENCER RA (1891–1959)

c. 1939, oil on paper, 40 × 28 cm
Wolverhampton Art Gallery and Museums
EXHIBITIONS: *Object of the Month*, Victoria and Albert Museum, London, July 1984

This small oil painting was used as the original design for a tapestry, 'Man with Cabbages', woven by the Dovecot Tapestry Co., Edinburgh, in 1949 and acquired by the Astor family. A related drawing is reproduced in Carolyn Leder, 'Stanley Spencer', *The Astor Collection*, London, 1976, no. 11.

The figures include a self-portrait of the artist as a boy threading conkers, and his friend Daphne Charlton as a girl exploring the bole of the tree. This is a characteristic poetic invention on Spencer's part; in fact they first met in March 1939. Spencer valued her friendship and support greatly, especially after the breakdown of his relationship with Patricia Preece. He stayed with Daphne and George Charlton at Leonard Stanley in Gloucestershire for twelve months from 1939 to 1940, and the painting probably dates from this period.

To mark the centenary of Wolverhampton Art Gallery in 1984, the Friends of the Art Gallery, a registered charity, launched an appeal to purchase this fine work by Stanley Spencer, priced at £16,000. They successfully raised £4,000 from local sources with the V&A Purchase Grant Fund offering a further £8,000. The NHMF were approached and offered a grant of £4,000 to secure the work for the Gallery.

43 *The Balcony at the Alhambra*

SPENCER FREDERICK GORE (1878–1914)

c. 1911–12, oil on canvas, 48.2 × 35.5 cm
York City Art Gallery
1384
EXHIBITIONS: *Object of the Month*, Victoria and Albert
Museum, London, February 1985; *Art in Performance,
Performance in Art*, Nottingham Castle Museum, 1987;
The Painters of Camden Town, Christie's, 1988

This painting depicts a famous music hall in Leicester Square
and is a key work in the history of the Camden Town Group.
This was a short-lived but highly significant alliance of artists
centred around Walter Sickert, working in London and exhibiting at the Carfax Gallery in the years 1911 and 1912. The
main protagonists apart from Sickert were Robert Bevan,
Harold Gilman, Charles Ginner and Spencer Gore. These
painters experimented with new techniques, particularly
those of the French Impressionists and Post-Impressionists,
making of them something very much their own, and, like
the French artists, they looked to contemporary urban life,
such as the music hall, for their subject matter.

In its daring composition and bold colour scheme the
painting reflects the particular influence of Gauguin, whose
work Gore would have seen at Roger Fry's exhibition *Manet
and the Post-Impressionists* held at the Grafton Galleries in the
winter of 1910 to 1911 and at the Gauguin and Cézanne
exhibition held at the Stafford Gallery in November 1911.
It has been described as 'a masterpiece of Gauguinesque
synthesis'.

York City Art Gallery has a small but important collection
of Camden Town Group paintings, largely as a result of the
generosity of the late Dean Milner-White. *The Balcony at the
Alhambra* (which formerly belonged to Lord Killanin) was an
appropriate addition, not least because it provides a splendid
example of a music hall subject, a theme which was of
particular interest to Gore and Sickert but not previously
represented at York.

The Gallery's annual acquisitions budget has been about
£2,000 for many years, whereas the cost of *The Balcony at the
Alhambra* was £16,200. Its purchase was made possible by a
grant of £4,050 from the NHMF together with contributions
from the V & A Purchase Grant Fund and the Friends of York
City Art Gallery.

43

44

44 *Spring: Apple Blossoms*

SIR JOHN EVERETT MILLAIS (1829–96)

1856–9, oil on canvas, 110.5 × 172.5 cm
*Trustees of the National Museums and Galleries on Merseyside
(Lady Lever Art Gallery, Port Sunlight)*
LLAG 3605

Millais conceived this picture as a pendant to *Autumn Leaves* (1855) and when it was eventually exhibited in 1859 it was under the title of *Spring* alone. Later it became familiar as *Apple Blossoms*. Millais's keenness to paint apple-trees in blossom, revealed in letters to his wife of the early summer of 1856, seems to have been the creative mainspring of the work. He thus anticipated the well-known passage in Ruskin's 1858 *Academy Notes*: 'how strange that among all this painting of delicate detail, there is not a true one of English spring! – that no Pre-Raphaelite has painted a cherry-tree in blossom . . . nor the flush of the apple blossom . . .' Ruskin's reaction to the picture at the Royal Academy in 1859 was nevertheless severe: he termed it a 'fierce and rigid orchard'; and 'an angry blooming (petals as it were of japanned brass)'. Other critics too reacted with ill-ease, agreeing on the coarseness of the painting.

With his other major exhibition pictures of the later 1850s, *Sir Isumbras* and *The Vale of Rest*, *Apple Blossoms* marks Millais's transition from Pre-Raphaelitism proper to his more popular style inaugurated with *The Black Brunswicker* (1860). Those transitional works, larger in format than previous exhibition pictures, introduce enigmatical subject matter and a more complex sequential and planar narrative technique in place of the single central image of earlier 1850s works. Their gestation period in each case was long and marked by self-doubt and technical fallibility. As perhaps the epitome of this phase, *Apple Blossoms* possesses a special place in the artist's work.

The painting was purchased from the Liverpool collection of Thomas Clarke in 1920 by the 1st Viscount Leverhulme, whose particular favourite Millais was. It descended in his family until offered for private treaty sale by the 3rd Viscount to the Trustees of the National Museums and Galleries on Merseyside in April 1986. The NHMF contributed £103,350 to the purchase price.

45 *Writing Cabinet*

CHARLES ROBERT ASHBEE (1863–1942) and the
GUILD OF HANDICRAFT LTD

c. 1902, mahogany carcass veneered in ebony and holly,
135 × 108 × 54.5 cm
Cheltenham Art Gallery and Museums
1982:194
EXHIBITIONS: *Beauty's Awakening*, Brighton, 1984

Surprise is a key element in the design of this writing cabinet: the dark and severely rectilinear cabinet opens to reveal a pale interior decorated with inlay of stylised flowers and pierced metal handles set against scarlet morocco leather.

The design is inspired by seventeenth-century pieces and especially by the Spanish cabinets known as *varguenos*, but it also shows the influence of M.H. Baillie Scott, for whom the Guild of Handicraft executed work in the late 1890s. It represents Ashbee's furniture design at its peak.

Ashbee worked in a range of media, all subordinated to his crusading zeal to foster the innate talents of the ordinary workers employed in the Guild of Handicraft, which he founded in London in 1888. The Guild transferred to Chipping Campden in 1902 and remained there until its financial collapse in 1907.

The cabinet seems to have been made as an exhibition piece and was on sale in 1903 at £80. It was eventually acquired by Rob Holland Martin, a Director of the Guild, was sold twice in the 1950s, and appeared at Sotheby's in 1981. Cheltenham Museum's excellent Arts and Crafts collection lacked any furniture by Ashbee and this was a rare opportunity to acquire a superb example. Generous grants were received from a number of bodies; the NHMF's assistance of £4,000 was crucial in securing the cabinet for Cheltenham at the auction at a price of £32,400.

46 *Weeping Woman*

PABLO PICASSO (1881–1973)

1937, oil on canvas, 59.7 × 48.9 cm
The Trustees of the Tate Gallery, London

Weeping Woman was painted by Picasso in October 1937, and is closely related in style and mood to his great mural *Guernica* which was completed a few months earlier. It is the culminating masterpiece in a series of studies of weeping women and at the same time is a portrait of his companion Dora Maar. It is one of Picasso's finest paintings of the 1930s and is among the most striking images of twentieth-century art.

Guernica, which was inspired by the bombing of the Basque town of that name in the Spanish Civil War, featured women as the innocent victims of aggression. Its sombre monochrome colours highlighted the symbolic nature of the image. In *Weeping Woman* Picasso concentrated on grief in its private form. Focusing on the head alone and using vivid colours, he achieved an effect of searing intensity. As Sir Roland Penrose, who bought the painting directly from Picasso in October 1937, has written: 'The result of using colour in a manner so totally unassociated with grief, for a face in which sorrow is evident in every line, is highly disconcerting. As though the tragedy had arrived with no warning, the red and blue hat is decked with a blue flower. The white handkerchief pressed to her face hides nothing of the agonised grimace on her lips: it serves merely to bleach her cheeks with the colour of death.'

The painting had been on loan to the Tate Gallery since 1969. In 1987, Antony Penrose offered the painting in lieu of taxes on his father's estate. However, the value of the painting exceeded the tax debt and under Treasury rules, the nation could not make up the difference. However, the Arts Minister agreed for the first time to combine a tax write-off with a cash payment. The NHMF were delighted to support this unique solution, and of the £1,915,000 needed by the Tate to secure the painting, NHMF gave a grant of £900,000.

45

46

47

48d

47 Douglas Douglas-Hamilton, 14th Duke of Hamilton, with Elizabeth, Duchess of Hamilton

OSKAR KOKOSCHKA (1886–1980)

1969, oil on canvas, 89.8 × 129.8 cm,
signed bottom left 'OK'
Scottish National Portrait Gallery, Edinburgh
PG 2723

This portrait was painted at Lennoxlove, the Duke of Hamilton's seat, during July 1969. Within the vibrancy of pigment and colour is a kind of alert melancholy, the Duke and Duchess offering each other support in face of the strange onslaught that Kokoschka's art must have seemed to them. As befits a Scottish nobleman, the Duke wears a kilt – it was Kokoschka who had insisted on this – while placed in the background on the right is one of the major historical family portraits, Gilbert Jackson's *John, Lord Belasyse of Worlaby* recently acquired by the National Portrait Gallery, London (see no. 49).

The commission was originally suggested to a bank, on whose board the Duke sat, by the sitters' son, Lord Hugh Douglas-Hamilton. The bank, however, lacked the courage which the Duke subsequently showed when he pursued the idea himself – and persisted in the face of Kokoschka's initial reaction: 'You do not want to be painted by me – my art is cruel!' The portrait can now be seen as a remarkably enlightened act of patronage, an immensely important link between Scotland and one of the major traditions of European painting.

Despite his gentle, even retiring, nature the Duke was in many ways a man of action. As the 'boxing Marquis' of Clydesdale he had won the Scottish amateur middleweight title in 1924, and in 1933 he had been chief pilot on the first flight over Mount Everest. In 1941 he was very briefly involved in the strange episode of the flight of Rudolph Hess to Scotland. He continued to serve in the Royal Air Force throughout the Second World War.

The portrait was on loan to the Scottish National Portrait Gallery and had come to look more and more at home in that setting. It was purchased in 1987, along with one of the most splendid of the Hamilton family portraits (Mytens's full-length of the 1st Duke), for a combined price of £440,000, of which £260,000 was contributed by the NHMF.

48 The Messel-Rosse Collection of Fans

a) Folding Fan, English, 1801 (M.216-1985)
Double paper leaf, printed and hand-coloured; pierced ivory sticks and guards.
Inscribed: 'Published as the Act directs by T. Cock, J.P. Crowder & Co., No. 21 Wood Street, Cheapside, London, Octo 2 1801'
The design features the twelve signs of the Zodiac. When held up to the light, two portrait medallions are visible between the two putti and the central vignette of Peace.

b) Chinese brisé fan, early 18th century (M.89-1984)
ivory, pierced, painted in red, green and gilt.
An early Chinese export fan, with concealed stringing instead of ribbon.

c) Folding Fan, Italian, c. 1720–30 (M.28-1985)
Double paper leaf painted in gouache; ivory sticks piqué in silver and inlaid with tortoiseshell, coloured ivory and engraved mother-of-pearl
The front is decorated with a lively *fête galante* and the reverse with a man and woman dancing in the open air.

d) Folding Fan, West European, probably German, c. 1750–60 (M.151-1985)
Single paper leaf, painted on gilt; pierced and painted ivory sticks; pierced ivory guards inlaid with mother-of-pearl.
This fan combines European subjects, *trompe-l'oeil* lace and floral sprays on the leaf with a chinoiserie decoration on the sticks.
The Syndics of the Fitzwilliam Museum, Cambridge

Wealthy collectors acquired fans from all over Europe on the Grand Tour; Horace Walpole's letters refer to choosing fans for friends in Paris, and Fanny Burney's diary to fan leaves being painted by Reynolds, Kauffman and Goupy.

The Messel-Rosse Collection of fans is the personal and private accumulation of one person, Leonard Messel, at the start of the twentieth century. The fans were never bought for use but purely for their rarity and historical background. The Collection is one of the largest in existence, amounting to almost five hundred fans ranging from the seventeenth to the late nineteenth century.

Leonard Messel collected European fans from England, France, Spain, the Italian states, the Germanic countries and north-west Europe. These include a unique seventeenth-century standing feather fan, fans of vellum, kid, paper and silk, embroidered fans, and fans painted and decorated with mica, mother-of-pearl, feathers and sequins. There are also fans from China, Japan, India, Indonesia and Korea, including folding fans painted in delicate watercolours, and lacquered ivory fans.

In 1984, the collection was offered to the Fitzwilliam Museum by the Countess of Rosse, in whose care the fans had been left, and the NHMF provided a grant of £79,843 to enable the Museum to purchase it.

49 John, Lord Belasyse of Worlaby

GILBERT JACKSON (fl. 1622–40)

Signed and dated 1636, oil on canvas, 189.2 × 129.5 cm
National Portrait Gallery, London
5948

Like his father Lord Fauconberg, Belasyse (1614–1689) was a staunch supporter of Charles I, and at the outbreak of the Civil War was one of the first to join the King at Oxford. A man 'of exemplary industry and courage', he raised at his own expense six regiments of horse and foot, and was rewarded with a peerage in 1645. He fought at Edgehill, Newbury and Naseby, and took part in the sieges of Reading, Bristol and Newark. At the Restoration his career was largely frustrated by his Roman Catholicism. Forced to resign the Governorship of Tangier, he was deeply implicated in Titus Oates's alleged Popish Plot in 1678, and spent six years as a prisoner in the Tower. He was released in 1684 on bail of £50,000 by James, Duke of York who, as James II, gave him his last public appointment, as First Commissioner of the Treasury.

This important portrait is one of the most attractive works

49

50

of the native painter Gilbert Jackson, whose portraits, despite Jackson's probable base in London, strike a boldly provincial note, untouched by the sophistication of Van Dyck. It was painted in the year of Belasyse's marriage to Jane, daughter of Sir Robert Boteler, and may well commemorate that event, for what must be her portrait is, most unusually, included in the background. The mood is one of youthful optimism, intensified by Belasyse's jaunty stance, the cheery colours, and the bold two-dimensional patterning.

The Gallery bought the portrait at Sotheby's on 15 July 1987 (lot 20) from the collection of the Dukes of Hamilton. It fetched £178,400, a record price for Jackson, and one beyond the Gallery's means. The NHMF made the purchase possible with a grant of £106,400, augmented by £22,000 from the NA-CF, and the Gallery raised the balance of £50,000. (See also no. 47)

50 *Horatio, Viscount Nelson*
SIR WILLIAM BEECHEY (1753–1839)

> 1800, oil on canvas, 62.3 × 48.3 cm
> *National Portrait Gallery, London*
> 5798

This vivid sketch by Beechey is for his large full-length portrait of Nelson commissioned by the City of Norwich in

1800. Beechey, Norfolk-born like Nelson, was given the commission shortly after Nelson returned home from the Mediterranean as the hero of the Battle of the Nile. Nelson is shown in rear-admiral's uniform with the Stars of the Bath, St Ferdinand and the Crescent, and two Naval Gold Medals (St Vincent and the Nile); the Nile scar is visible over his right eye. The vividness and directness of the portrait provide an image of the great Admiral as close and faithful as we are likely to see.

The sketch appears to have remained in the possession of the descendants of the family of the artist until it was sold in 1966. It was bought by Hugh Leggatt who placed it on loan to the National Portrait Gallery until 1985 when it was purchased by the Gallery by private treaty sale with a contribution of £100,000 from the NHMF.

51 *The Mostyn Tompion Clock*
THOMAS TOMPION (1639–1713)

> London, c. 1690, ebony veneered oak with mounts of silver and gilded brass, height 71 cm, width 33 cm, depth 24 cm
> *The Trustees of the British Museum*
> M&LA. 1982,7-2, 1

The dome of the clock bears the Royal coat of arms and

Britannia with a shield bearing the combined crosses of St George and St Andrew. At the corners are the rose (for England), the thistle (for Scotland) and the lion and unicorn (the Royal Supporters). Other mounts include emblematic crossed sceptres with crowns, military trophies and lion masks. The pendulum and the movement signature 'Tho Tompion London Fecit' are visible through the glazed aperture.

The gilded brass dial has a silvered chapter-ring and silver spandrels; the hands are of blued steel. The days of the week and their corresponding planets are shown in the apertures. A silver plaque bears the signature 'T Tompion Londini Fecit'.

Year duration is achieved by the use of trains of six wheels accommodated between two sets of plates and driven by massive great wheels and spring barrels. The going train has a verge escapement and short pendulum. A quarter repeat mechanism with two bells can be operated by pulling a cord at either side of the case, enabling the time to be ascertained during hours of darkness.

In 1680 Tompion had become London's leading clock-maker, in terms of both quantity and quality. During the last thirty years of the seventeenth century, when England pioneered a revolution in the mechanical keeping of time, he stood out as the most inventive of all his contemporaries.

The clock is believed to have been commissioned in 1689, the year of the coronation of Mary (daughter of James II) and William of Orange. Indeed, the coat of arms is as borne for a few months in the summer of 1689, although it was also occasionally used, erroneously, at later dates. However, no record of payment for the clock appears in the Royal Treasury Books unless, for some reason, delivery was delayed until 1693, during which year Tompion was paid the vast sum of £600 for 'a fine clock'. It may be significant that the payment is preceded by one of £50 to Daniel Marot who is thought to have designed the case and its mounts.

On the death of William III in 1702 the clock was part of the legacy of 'the contents of the King's Bedchamber' which passed to Henry Sydney, Earl Romney, who was Gentleman of the Bedchamber and Groom of the Stole. It then passed by descent to the 5th Lord Mostyn, from whom it was purchased by the Trustees of the British Museum. They were assisted by funds bequeathed by Mrs Katherine Goodhart Kitchingman and, above all, by a grant from the NHMF of £250,000. Without this grant the Museum would not have been able to acquire the clock, one of the great technical *tours de force* of European horology.

52   *The Marlborough Ice Pails*

> *c.* 1685–95, 22-carat gold, weight 11.4 kg, height 26.9 cm
> diameter of rim 21.8 cm
> *The Trustees of the British Museum, London*
> M&LA 1981, 12-1 and 2

This pair of ice pails has a restrained degree of chased ornament that strikes a skilful balance with the powerful simplicity of their massive forms. A reeded moulding and incised lines divide the body into two zones, the upper being plain except for the moulded lip and two vigorous baroque lion-masks and elegant hinged handles. The lower zone is

51. Illustrated in colour, title-page.

52. Also illustrated on p. 25.

enriched with alternating long and short fluting that spirals to the right and terminates in a large curling foliate motif and a triple scale motif. The low spreading foot is similarly decorated but on a smaller scale and, because it spirals in the reverse direction, an effective sense of contrast has been created.

Like most gold plate of the seventeenth century, these ice pails bear no marks but, on stylistic grounds, can be reliably dated between 1685 and 1695, and are, therefore, the earliest known examples of this important new form of European plate. The ice pail – as distinct from the cistern or wine-cooler that stood on the floor – made its appearance on the Continent early in the 1680s, becoming popular at the French court of Louis XIV and being almost immediately copied in London.

Being made of gold, the Marlborough ice pails have not diminished in weight nor suffered any loss of definition through cleaning since their weight was first recorded on the death of the celebrated Sarah, 1st Duchess of Marlborough, in 1744. They were kept in 'the Iron Chest' at the London home of the Marlboroughs and an early list of gold and silver plate signed by Sarah on 18 May 1712 has a brief entry that seems to refer to them. The ice pails belong to those momentous years when the great John Churchill's career was in the ascendancy and, through him, England's contribution to international politics became a crucial factor. He died in 1722 but the ice pails, like the Marlborough Ambassadorial Plate which King William III had delivered to him in 1701, were bequeathed by Sarah in 1744 to her grandson John, the younger brother of the new Duke.

Consequently, the ice pails remained at Althorp, carefully preserved by the Earls Spencer, until 1982 when they were purchased by the British Museum with a generous grant of £140,000 from the NHMF and donations from the NA-CF, the Worshipful Company of Goldsmiths, the Pilgrim Trust and with funds bequeathed by Mrs Katherine Goodhart Kitchingman.

53 The Bodendick Candlesticks
JACOB BODENDICK (fl. c. 1660–88)

London, c. 1665, silver-gilt, height 24.5 cm
The Trustees of the Victoria and Albert Museum, London
M.261a-c-1984

Each of this pair of silver-gilt candlesticks bears the maker's mark of Jacob Bodendick (IB over a crescent). He was a native of Limburg who married the daughter of a London goldsmith in 1661 and became one of the alien goldsmiths supplying the court of Charles II. The sockets and drippans are formed as

53

clustered columns, and the bases, which are richly chased and embossed with acanthus, echo their 'Gothic' ogee form. An unusual feature, concealed in normal use, is a coat of arms engraved on the base of one of the sockets; the arms are those of George Tooke of Hertfordshire (d. 1662) and his second wife Anne Conningsbury. This is an instance of the goldsmith's practice of reusing old plate, which is rarely documented.

The Restoration coincided with a marked increase in the use of silver candlesticks, as part of the English response to French domestic refinements. Not only the aristocracy but also institutions and the bourgeoisie (Samuel Pepys for one) expected to use silver, rather than pewter, candlesticks. This pair is a rare survivor of the richly embossed silver of the 1660s; most of Bodendick's candlesticks date from the following decade, when the rich acanthus ornament was replaced by plainer forms.

These candlesticks are the first examples of the work of this important court goldsmith to be acquired for a national museum; they were purchased in 1984 by private treaty with a grant of £55,000 from the NHMF.

54 *The Portland Font*

PAUL STORR (1771–1844)

Hallmarked London 1797–8, 22-carat gold, weight
6.9 kg, pedestal 34.9 cm square,
diameter of bowl 21.6 cm
The Trustees of the British Museum
M&LA 1986,4-3,1

The Portland font survives with its integral square plinth covered in pale grey silk velvet and its four silver-gilt acanthus-leaf and ring handles. The burnished gold pedestal, with its plain mantled cartouche at the front, stands on four short tapering legs and supports the detachable christening bowl, which rests on four winged cherub feet and is flanked on three sides by the free-standing figures representing Faith, Hope and Charity.

Fully hallmarked in London in the year 1797–8, the Portland font is also struck with the mark of Paul Storr (1771–1844). His training is obscure and this brilliantly executed and finely chased font is the earliest major work of importance bearing Storr's mark. It is not yet clear how he obtained this grand and highly prestigious commission but Humphry Repton (1752–1818) claimed in his book, *Observations on the Theory and Practice of Landscape Gardening*, 1803, not only to be the author of the design of the Portland font but also to have

54. Illustrated in colour on p. 22.

given it 'to the goldsmith' (un-named). In design, it is the earliest example in English Neo-classical goldsmiths' work of the use of free-standing sculptural figures.

Humphry Repton also offers confirmation that the font was made for the 3rd Duke of Portland to present to his son, the Marquess of Titchfield, on the birth of his first son, who was christened on 29 September 1796. The 3rd Duke (1738–1809) was twice Prime Minister and, at the time, was Home Secretary (1794–1801) and Chancellor of the University of Oxford. No other gold font for private use in England has been recorded and this unique survival, which has descended in the one family, is in excellent condition. Being executed in gold, the crispness and detail of the font have suffered no loss through cleaning and, consequently, the subtle chasing of the figures, sculptural works of a high order by a gifted but unidentified modeller, is unimpaired.

Sold at Christie's by Lady Anne Bentinck on 11 July 1985, the font became the subject of an export licence application but its national importance was established and the font was purchased by the British Museum with a grant of £900,000 from the NHMF and with funds bequeathed by George Bernard Shaw.

55 Thirteen 'Apostle' Spoons

London, 1536–1537, silver, average length 19.5 cm
The Trustees of the British Museum, London
MLA 1981, 7-1, 1-13

These thirteen silver spoons have hexagonal stems and 'apostle' finials representing (upper row, left to right): Simon Zelotes, with a saw, James the Greater, dressed as a pilgrim, Peter, his sword and key missing, the Virgin Mary, John, the Evangelist, holding a cup, his book missing, Andrew, with a diagonal cross, Jude, with a long cross; and (lower row): probably Thomas, his spear and book missing, Matthias, with an axe, probably Paul, with a sword and book, James the Less, with a fuller's bat, probably Bartholomew, his knife missing, and Matthew, with a carpenter's square. The bowl of each spoon has been engraved (before the assay) with the 'Sacred Monogram', *ihs*. The stems are struck with the London date-letter T for 1536–37 and an unidentified maker's mark which is difficult to interpret but could be a sheaf of corn. The bowls are struck with a leopard's head. There is gilding (covering old damage) on the finials and traces of gilding on the engraved roundel and punch-mark in the bowls. Each spoon has been engraved on the back of the bowl with an anchor, the crest of Thomas Bruges (d. 1835).

Spoons with the apostle finials were popular in England from the fifteenth century to the mid-seventeenth. They were frequently made in sets showing the twelve apostles and

55 (detail). Finial representing St Andrew.

56

Christ; the only other sixteenth-century set of thirteen still complete is now in California. This set is unique in having the Virgin Mary in place of Christ.

The goldsmith who made the finials made use of models of exceptional sculptural quality. Three of the finials (James the Greater, Peter, and John) are similar to figures adorning the magnificent crozier (at Corpus Christi College, Oxford) of Richard Fox, Bishop of Winchester. The crozier was probably made around 1501, or rather earlier; so the models were of some age when used for the spoons.

The spoons belonged to the Long family of Wiltshire by 1611. They were then given by Katherine Long (1717–1814) to her steward Thomas Bruges, before passing by descent to the Ludlow-Bruges family of Seend, Wiltshire. They were sold at Christie's on 16 July 1903 for £4,900, and acquired by William Waldorf Astor of Hever Castle. Having been sold again at Christie's on 24 June 1981 (lot 104) they were subsequently purchased by the British Museum for a price of £150,000 with the aid of the first NHMF grant (of £75,000) to the Museum.

56 The Trenchard Bowl

Chinese, Jiajing period (1522–1566), porcelain in silver-gilt mounts; mounts London hallmark 1599, maker's mark 'IH' in shaped shield (overstriking another), height 13 cm
The Trustees of the Victoria and Albert Museum, London
M. 945-1983

This Chinese porcelain bowl descended in the Trenchard family and was reputedly a gift with other objects to Sir Thomas Trenchard, Sheriff of Dorset, from Joanna the Mad and Philip of Austria, who received hospitality at Wolfeton House after they were shipwrecked off Weymouth in 1506. Given the importance of this episode in the history of the Trenchard family, it is hardly surprising that this tradition attached itself to an object as exotic as this bowl. However, the porcelain was made more than half a century after Joanna's visit and the mounts are the work of a late Elizabethan goldsmith.

Small quantities of Chinese export porcelain were reaching England in the late sixteenth century. Its rarity and the high status it enjoyed at court is evident both from references in the gift lists of Elizabeth I and from the quality of the goldsmith's work on the two surviving objects; most are buffet pieces, ewers and basins mounted for display like this one. The largest group of display porcelain with Elizabethan mounts was formerly at Burghley House (now in the Metropolitan Museum of Art, New York); the design of the handles and carotid straps are close to those of the Trenchard bowl, suggesting a common workshop source for the models or casting patterns.

The Trenchard bowl descended in the Trenchard and Lane families and was placed on loan to the Victoria and Albert Museum by a descendant in 1976. In 1983, just before it was to be withdrawn for sale at auction, a private treaty purchase was negotiated. The NHMF gave a grant of £55,000 towards its purchase.

57 *Order of St Patrick*

a) Collar: *c.* 1830, silver-gilt with enamel decoration,
length 148 cm;
b) Knight's Badge: *c.* 1845, gold, enamel and agate
The Trustees of the Ulster Museum, Belfast

Apart from the official Collar, which was presented to a Knight on his admission and had to be returned on his death, most of the regalia of the Order of St Patrick was provided by the members themselves. Private copies of the splendid Collar, however, were sometimes retained as family heirlooms. This one is of silver-gilt with seven roses enamelled alternately white petals within red and red petals within white. The oval Knight's Badge, in gold, enamel and agate, with a three-colour cameo on the reverse, is considered to be the finest surviving example of its type.

The Most Illustrious Order of St Patrick, which ranked along with the Garter and the Thistle as one of the three major orders of knighthood, was founded in 1783 by George III and, although never officially disbanded, effectively came to an end in 1922 with the foundation of the Irish Free State. The monarch was Sovereign of the Order, the Lord Lieutenant of Ireland its Grand Master. The number of Knights was strictly limited, at first to fifteen, later, from 1821, to twenty-two. As the country's rarest honour (in the Order's entire history there were fewer than two hundred Knights), the KP was eagerly sought by the Anglo–Irish aristocracy. The so-called crown jewels of Ireland, mysteriously stolen from Dublin Castle in 1907, largely consisted of St Patrick regalia.

Both Collar and Knight's Badge were purchased by the Ulster Museum at Christie's in 1983, at a time when the Museum was receiving no annual purchase grant, for £17,000, all of which was provided by the NHMF. The Museum was thus able to complete its collection of major items of the Order's regalia.

57

58 (front); illustrated in colour, frontispiece.

58 (back)

58 *Beilby Goblet*
Decoration by WILLIAM BEILBY (1740–1819)

Signed BEILBY JUNr INV^T S PINX^T
Probably 1762, enamel on glass, height 25 cm
Whitehaven Museum
WHHMG 1985 500
EXHIBITIONS: Corning Museum of Glass, USA,
16 October 1987–16 October 1988

This 'slave trade' goblet is clearly related to several other goblets enamelled by William Beilby, all of which bear the royal arms of George III. However, it differs from the others in two important respects: it is somewhat larger, and instead of the 'Prince of Wales feathers' motif on the reverse, a sailing vessel is depicted, under the legend 'Success to the African Trade of Whitehaven'. In common with only two other 'Royal' goblets extant it is signed by the artist.

It is believed that these goblets were made in 1762 to commemorate the birth of the future King George IV. The 'slave trade' variant may have been made slightly later as it is believed to have been commissioned to mark the launch at

Whitehaven of a vessel called the *King George* for the slave trade in May 1763. Although in the eighteenth and nineteenth centuries Whitehaven was an important shipbuilding port, the *King George* was one of only two vessels specifically built for the slave trade.

The goblet has a curious connection with John Paul Jones, often known as the 'Father of the American Navy'. Born at Kirkbean on the Scottish side of the Solway, John Paul, who did not assume the surname Jones until some years later, was apprenticed to a Whitehaven merchant called John Younger. Part-way through his apprenticeship his master 'failed in business' and released him from his indentures. He also used his influence to obtain for this promising youth the post of Third Mate aboard the *King George* on her maiden slave voyage. It is probable then, that 'America's Nelson' would have sipped from this goblet during the launching ceremony at Whitehaven.

The goblet was purchased by Whitehaven Museum at public auction on 5 June 1985 for a hammer price of £56,160, with the aid of a grant of £8,098 from the NHMF.

59 *The 'Margaret and Winneford' Bowl*
Decoration attributed to WILLIAM BEILBY
(1740–1819)

1767, enamel on glass, height 11.5 cm,
diameter 24 cm
Tyne and Wear Museums Service (Laing Art Gallery)

The bowl is a charming example of the enamelled glass associated with the Beilby family of Newcastle upon Tyne. The thickly blown glass is delicately painted in coloured enamels with a decorative border of diapers, swags and scrolls; the arms of the Forster family within a rococo shield; a picture of the ship *The Margaret and Winneford*; and, in the base of the bowl, a white swan.

William, Ralph and Thomas Beilby made their living in Newcastle during the 1760s by practising 'a variety of arts of a curious and unusual nature', including metal engraving, seal cutting and enamelling on glass. William and Thomas were also drawing masters. This bowl was probably decorated to celebrate the launching of *The Margaret and Winneford* in April 1767. The Forster arms refer to Henry Forster of Gateshead who built and part-owned the ship.

The bowl, which had passed by descent through the family until 1970, was placed on loan to the Laing Art Gallery in 1973, where it formed the centrepiece of the Gallery's display of Beilby glass. In 1984 the owner removed the bowl and sent it for auction in London where it was sold to an American private collector. Fortunately, an export licence was deferred and within three months Tyne and Wear Museums Service, with the help of a grant of £2,500 from the NHMF, was able to buy the bowl for £28,000. The bowl has now returned to the Laing Art Gallery.

60

60 The Travelling Service of Princess Pauline Borghese

Supplied by MARTIN-GUILLAUME BIENNAIS (1764–1843)

Probably assembled *c.* 1803–1804, mahogany, silver-gilt, glass, mother-of-pearl and other materials,
case 18.8 × 57.3 × 40 cm
The Trustees of the National Museums of Scotland, Edinburgh
1986.5
EXHIBITIONS: *French Connections: Scotland and the Arts of France*, Edinburgh International Festival, 1985

This great *nécessaire de voyage*, containing items for the *toilette*, meals and writing, is a development of travelling services owned by Queen Marie-Antoinette and other important ladies associated with the court of Louis XVI.

Its creator, Biennais, began as a *tabletier* (a person who makes or sells small items of wood, ivory and tortoiseshell) and became a specialist assembler-supplier of travelling services. Patronised by Napoleon, he became his official goldsmith when he was First Consul and later Emperor. At one stage demand was so great that Biennais is said to have employed six hundred workers in various materials.

Princess Pauline Borghese (1780–1825), the favourite sister of Emperor Napoleon, probably acquired the *nécessaire* around the time of her marriage to Prince Camillo Borghese, in 1803. After her brother's downfall, she settled in Rome where she formed a relationship with Alexander, later 10th Duke of Hamilton (1767–1852), an ardent admirer of Napoleon. In her will, Pauline bequeathed the service to the Duke as 'a mark of my friendship'.

The National Museums of Scotland were anxious to secure the Borghese *nécessaire* in order to develop their important collection of French silver (which includes the famous Lennoxlove toilet service and one half of the Napoleon tea service of 1810) and to illustrate the 10th Duke of Hamilton's interest in Napoleon. Alexander was the greatest collector in the history of Scotland and the man most responsible for forming the celebrated Hamilton Palace Collection. Inspired by the bequest of the *nécessaire*, he went on to commission Napoleon's former designer Charles Percier to prepare designs for the interior of the new north block of Hamilton Palace, to purchase the magnificent Napoleon tea service of 1810, and even to marry his son and heir to a relative of the late Emperor.

The NHMF contributed £390,000 towards the private treaty price of £620,000. The *nécessaire* is on display in the Royal Museum of Scotland, Edinburgh.

61 Staffordshire Knife Case

1765–70, enamel on copper with gilt-metal mounts,
height 25.2 cm, width 18.2 cm, depth 13 cm
Bantock House Museum, Wolverhampton
Cat. No. 690/1–25

This Staffordshire enamel knife case contains twelve knives and twelve forks with silver mounts and enamel handles. The interior is lined with dark pink velvet on a wood frame, with silver braid strips defining the compartments for the knives and forks, which are stored vertically. The exterior is decorated with two landscape scenes, birds and floral sprays.

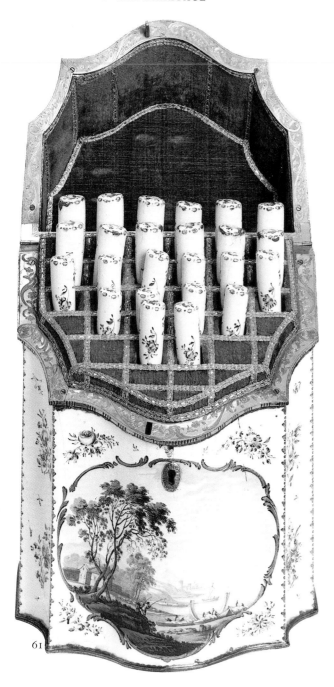

61

of decorative art formed by the late Tom Burn at Rous Lench Court in Worcestershire. With the dispersal of the greater part of these collections at auction in July 1986, the assistance of the NHMF and other organisations was sought by the Museum to keep a unique English eighteenth-century enamel in this country, where it could be viewed by the public. The total cost was £34,565, towards which the NHMF contributed £10,600.

62   *The Lazarus Collection of Glass*

a) Drinking glass
    c. 1730, round funnel bowl on Silesian stem and folded foot, wheel-engraved with allegorical figure and motto 'HAEC LIBERTATIS ERGO' (these things mean Liberty)
b) Drinking glass
    c. 1745, mould-blown bowl on double-series air-twist stem
c) Deceptive glass
    c. 1770, mould-blown bowl on double-series opaque-twist stem. (The thickened walls of the bowl reduce its capacity and have led to similar glasses being called 'toastmaster's glasses': a toast-master was expected to remain sober no matter how many toasts he had to drink.)
Bristol Museum and Art Gallery

Peter Lazarus, former headmaster of a preparatory school near Bristol, built up an important collection of glass. 164 were purchased by Bristol Museum, and these date from the period 1680 to 1810 when English glass-making enjoyed a high reputation at home and abroad. The pieces illustrate the wide variety of bowl shapes and stem types produced. The earliest glasses still show Venetian influence, but were soon superseded by the heavy baluster-stemmed glasses of the early eighteenth century which, with their simple shapes, demonstrate the brilliance of English lead glass.

From the second quarter of the eighteenth century, plain stems often enclose an air or opaque enamel twist, while bowls become noticeably smaller and are often ornamented. The Lazarus Collection includes examples of gilding, enamelling and both wheel and stipple engraving. The engraved decoration provides a fascinating insight into eighteenth-century political and social life. In addition to the inevitable Jacobite glasses there are glasses supporting various monarchs, political factions and parliamentary candidates. On a more intimate scale, a number of glasses commemorate individuals or illustrate scenes from contemporary life, most usually hunting or drinking.

The city of Bristol is famous throughout the world for its glass-making industry in the eighteenth and early nineteenth centuries, and the Museum and Art Gallery has important collections of documentary Bristol pieces and of the various coloured glass which was once, optimistically, associated with the city. The acquisition of the Lazarus glasses has added a new dimension to the collections by providing a wider view of British glass-making in the eighteenth century.

The Collection was purchased in 1984 for £91,310, with a grant of £11,153 from the NHMF. Financial assistance was also received from the V & A Purchase Grant Fund, the NA-CF and the Friends of Bristol Art Gallery.

Knife cases in the eighteenth century were usually made in wood and frequently in pairs; this single enamel example is a rarity, although knives and forks with enamel handles have survived as separate items. Other than from the south Staffordshire enamelling centres, it is not known exactly where or by whom the case was made, but it is almost certainly the work of an enameller who made the body, a mount-maker who would have made and supplied the mounts and handle, and perhaps two painters, one specialising in landscape scenes and the other in birds and flowers.

The knife case was one item among a fine collection of enamels which in turn comprised a part of the vast collection

62b, c and a

Portraits of Nature

FRED HOLLIDAY

From earliest times man has taken an interest in wildlife that has gone far beyond the utilitarian *eat it or be eaten by it*. Cave paintings made by early man in Europe, Africa and Australia demonstrate both artistic talent and an understanding of the lives of the creatures depicted. These early artists must have experienced feelings that were later shared by Landseer and Thomas Bewick as they carried out their work.

The theme of 'Man in Nature' was often chosen by landscape artists. Awe-inspiring views of rocks, crags and raging torrents were presented along with tiny human figures in order to emphasise, by comparison, the insignificance and vulnerability of mankind. Other artists turned to still-waters and cattle to depict a depth of peace and placidity, the very antithesis of wild nature. Sometimes the gods of nature were portrayed, hinting at a long-persistent folk memory of an early religion, and recent writers such as H H Munro (Saki) can still evoke a similar and surprisingly disquieting memory in his short stories such as *The Music on the Hill*.

A rich collection of countryside literature has emerged from the British Isles. Gilbert White's *Natural History of Selborne* is both scientific and popular. Richard Jefferies painted with words, as did Henry Williamson. As an inspiration to the poet, wildlife must rank alongside love and valour as a prime source.

The beginnings of the conservation movement are easy to find: when the British countryside was being dramatically changed by the industrial and agricultural revolutions it was not without its defenders. Robert Burns (a countryside writer with more than a common man's insight into nature) railed in poetry against the Duke of Queensberry who had destroyed the woods on the banks of the River Nith. But more often social position, affluence and leisure were the pre-requisites for the appreciation and protection of wildlife. If the 'shooting naturalist', such as Charles St John, is unacceptable today, remember that before the days of the telephoto lens to shoot, stuff, and draw and paint were the only sure ways of obtaining an identification of a bird or mammal. Tunnicliffe's sketchbooks show how much detail can be captured with pen and ink. Man in his time has been a hunter and a farmer; he has become urbanised and industrialised. In each of those phases he has dramatically altered the land and its plants and animals. The early discovery that some species could be brought under control drew the distinction immediately between domestic and wild. The latter were to be persecuted if they diminished man's property – so pests and weeds were identified. Those value judgements have been reinforced in stories, with good species and bad, perhaps nowhere better illustrated than in the children's stories of Beatrix Potter, who was also a fine wildlife artist.

While the beauty of wildlife is admired, it is also exploited for commercial gain and it is the practical and emotional aspects of conservation which serve to check against such abuse.

63. Cowslip, *Primula Veris*.

63. Barnacle Geeese on Islay, Scotland.

63 *Wildlife photographs*

These photographs show a variety of wildlife species, the protection of which is the primary aim of nature conservation. Individual animals and plants can survive only if they find the right habitats in which to feed and breed. As caterpillars many of our most beautiful butterflies need stinging nettles; without ponds and ditches there would be few dragonflies and no frogspawn. These habitats need to be cared for. We have lost too many hedges, too many old woodlands, too much downland, too many old pastures and orchards. They were lost because more people required more of life's necessities and luxuries; more houses, more factories, more roads. Our search for quality and quantity in agriculture has led to a greater use of pesticides. The land is in the grip of powerful machines and chemicals and wildlife is being squeezed to the margins. The County Naturalist Trusts, the Scottish Wildlife Trust, the National Trusts and the Royal Society for the Protection of Birds are but a few of the bodies that exist to own and manage habitats and to safeguard species at egg, seed, juvenile and adult stage. The Nature Conservancy Council and the two Countryside Commissions advise the government and the NHMF on the best policies and practices for the conservation of wildlife and scenery; happily, attractive landscape and rich wildlife usually go together.

Wildlife and countryside are a fundamental part of our heritage, since they have inspired some of our greatest writers and artists. As Robert Burns puts it: *I never hear the loud solitary whistle of the curlew in summer noon, or the wild mixing cadence of a troop of grey plover in an autumnal morning without feeling an elevation of soul like the enthusiasm of devotion or poetry.*

64 *Gibside from the South*

JOSEPH MALLORD WILLIAM TURNER RA
(1775–1851)

c. 1817, watercolour on paper, 27 × 43.7 cm
The Bowes Museum, Barnard Castle, Co. Durham
1983.35

65 *Gibside from the North*

JOSEPH MALLORD WILLIAM TURNER RA
(1775–1851)

c. 1817, watercolour on paper, 27.2 × 44.9 cm
The Bowes Museum, Barnard Castle, Co. Durham
1985.10

These watercolours were the result of a commission in 1817 to Turner from Robert Surtees, the great historian of County Durham, for an engraving to illustrate Surtees' history of the county.

Gibside estate, Co. Durham, came to the Bowes family following the marriage of Sir William Bowes to Elizabeth Blakiston, heiress to Gibside, in 1689. With great resources at their disposal, the Bowes family spent lavishly on buildings, furniture, silver, books and paintings. A stretch of the Derwent Valley was landscaped into a park and several structures were built to offset the natural landscape. These included the Chapel by James Paine (commissioned 1759), and the Column to British Liberty (1750–57), which were both depicted by Turner in *Gibside from the South*.

In 1777, George Bowes' only daughter and heiress, Mary

64

65

Eleanor Bowes, married, as her second husband a thorough rascal, Andrew Robinson Stoney, known as Stoney Bowes. Fortunately, the family fortune had been put in trust, so in order to raise money for his own purposes Stoney Bowes cut down many trees at Gibside, including a fine avenue, the remains of which is recorded by Turner. (The story of this marriage was to provide W.M. Thackeray with inspiration for his novel *Barry Lyndon*, in the 1840's.)

Once Turner had completed the watercolours, they were purchased by the then owner of Gibside, John, 10th Earl of Strathmore. They were inherited by his son, John Bowes, the founder of The Bowes Museum. *Gibside from the South* was sold at auction in July 1983 by the 17th Earl of Strathmore, and bought by The Bowes Museum for £58,630. The NHMF gave the Museum a grant of £16,630. *Gibside from the North* was auctioned in November 1983 and was acquired by Agnew's by arrangement with The Bowes Museum. Agnew's most generously held it until April 1984 when grants became available. The NHMF gave The Bowes Museum a grant of £9,000 towards the purchase of the companion watercolour.

66   *Watercolours of Fungi*

BEATRIX POTTER (1866–1943)

a) *Boletus scaber*
   30 September 1897
   8/151 A
b) *Clitocybe ampla*
   30 August 1895, inscribed 'Hermitage. Strath Braan'
   8/73
c) *Agaricus augustus*
   3 August 1895
   5/112
d) *Tapesia aurata*
   October 1896, inscribed 'Lakefield, Sawrey', and 'on dead spruce or scotch. fir'
   8/205
   Armitt Trust Collection, Ambleside

The four drawings are from the largest collection of Beatrix Potter's fungi watercolours and other studies which belong to the Armitt Trust in Ambleside. They were given by the artist herself to the Armitt Library and Museum of which she was a member. They date from an earlier period than her children's books. In the 1880s and 1890s, as an amateur scientist of rare skill and perception, Beatrix Potter was producing exquisite studies of natural history subjects all drawn to scale. These include mosses, lichens (of whose symbiotic compound nature she was one of the first to be aware), fossils, Roman antiquities and above all fungi and thick portfolios of her microscope studies. Among the microscope studies are her original observations of spore growth × 600 as drawn for her paper 'On the Germination of the Spores of the Agaricineae' read to the Linnaean Society in 1897 by George Masee FLS, ladies not then being expected to attend. Although contemporary experts failed to recognise the quality and significance of her work her observations have since been proved correct. Copies of these drawings were shown before the British Mycological Society in 1980 and the consensus of opinion was that Beatrix Potter had made accurate records and drawings of the spore germination and demonstrated how the spores were borne.

66c

Many of these drawings were, unfortunately, made on paper laminated onto poor quality board made of wood pulp which has been rendered acidic due to the presence of lignin. Others, on single sheets of paper have, with time, produced some localised stains or 'foxing'. A conservation programme was therefore urgently needed in order to prevent further deterioration of the watercolours. In 1986 the NHMF made available a grant of up to £1,000 to enable the Armitt Trust to begin the necessary conservation work.

67   *Wood Engravings*

THOMAS BEWICK (1753–1828)

a) *General History of Quadrupeds*, first edition, 1790
b) *History of British Birds*, vol. I, first edition, 1797
c) *A Pretty Book of Pictures for Little Masters and Misses: or, Tommy Trip's History of Beasts and Birds*, 1778
d) *New Lottery Book of Birds and Beasts for Children*, 1771
e) *Select Fables in Three Parts*, 1784
Bewick Birthplace Trust, Cherryburn, Northumberland

Bewick was apprenticed at the age of fourteen to Ralph Beilby, and was trained to handle every kind of engraving on metal and wood. For the following two years he worked from home on his own account, and then briefly in London. Soon he returned to Newcastle and for the following twenty years worked in partnership with his old master.

Besides a massive output of commercial work, Bewick published two major natural history books, the *General*

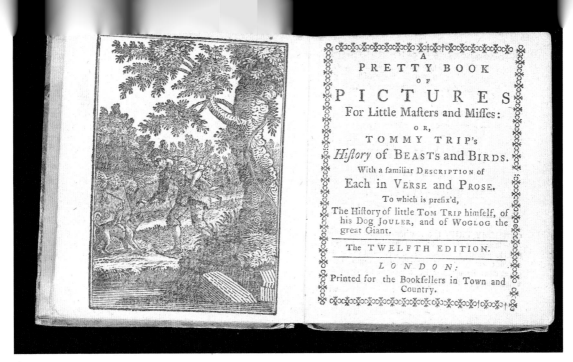

67c

68

History of Quadrupeds, 1790, and the *History of British Birds*, 1797 and 1804. Forced into semi-retirement by ill-health at the age of fifty-nine, Bewick left his only son Robert to manage the day-to-day business while he concentrated on the designs for his last completed book, the *Fables of Aesop*, published in 1817. In his final years he wrote a delightful autobiography which has since become a minor classic.

Bewick's reputation as an artist-engraver on wood brought him a fame in his lifetime which has never diminished. He had a particular genius for expressing in miniature form, often with pathos or humour, his deeply felt affection and understanding of the manners and scenes of north-country life, and the clarity of his observation was expressed with a virtuosity never since equalled. He is now universally acknowledged as the father of English wood engraving. His skill brought respectability to the medium and changed the course of book illustration for the remainder of the nineteenth century.

Bewick's birthplace at Cherryburn, near Newcastle, has recently been opened to the public as a museum. The NHMF gave a grant of £36,361 in 1984 to enable the Bewick Birthplace Trust to buy back over 150 of Bewick's original blocks engraved for the *Birds*, *Quadrupeds* and *Fables*. In 1987 the NHMF gave the Trust a further grant of £75,000 to enable the Trust to purchase an important library of books, particularly strong in the very rare children's books of his apprentice days. Both of these significant collections have returned to this country from America.

68 *A Wooded Landscape with Cattle by a Pool*
THOMAS GAINSBOROUGH (1727–88)

Exhibited 1792, oil on canvas, 120.4 × 147.6 cm
The Trustees of Gainsborough's House Society
1988. 1

Although drawing imaginary landscapes was one of Gainsborough's private relaxations from painting portraits, he exhibited his landscape paintings with pride. The brilliantly clear canvases of his native Suffolk countryside had given way to invention once he moved from East Anglia to Bath late in 1759. The West Country was rich in collections of Old Master paintings and, in a letter of 1768 to the actor David Garrick, Gainsborough recommends that his friend calls '. . . *upon any pretence* . . . at the Duke of Montagu's . . . to see his Grace's Landscape of Rubens'. In London, ten years later, Gainsborough was equally impressed by another landscape that belonged to Sir Joshua Reynolds. Rubens's *Landscape by Moonlight* (Princes Gate Collection, Courtauld Institute Galleries) inspired Gainsborough to paint a comparable, though larger, landscape with silhouetted animals at sunset. The painting was shown at the Royal Academy in 1782, when the Reverend Sir Henry Bate-Dudley described the landscape as Gainsborough's '. . . *chef d'oeuvre* in this line . . . that would have done honor to the most brilliant *Claude Lorain*!'.

The painting was next mentioned in the sale of Joseph Gillott in 1872 when it was bought by the London dealers Agnew's for Kirkham D. Hodgson. Some seventeen years later it was bought back and became part of Lord Iveagh's great collection. It hung in Grosvenor Place and remained in the family until it was offered for sale at Sotheby's in July

1987. After failing to meet its reserve, the painting was purchased net of capital tax by Suffolk County Council and transferred to Gainsborough's House Society. The £352,243 needed for the purchase was met with the help of a grant of £217,452 from the NHMF.

69 *Autograph manuscript of* The Natural History of Selborne
GILBERT WHITE (1720–93)

Folio, 193 leaves
The Gilbert White Museum, Selborne, Hampshire

Gilbert White's account of the natural history of his native village, first published in 1789, has been established for many years as a classic of both natural history writing and of English literature. The book is based upon two series of letters to fellow naturalists, Thomas Pennant (1727–1800) and the Hon. Daines Barrington (1726–98), written between 1767 and 1781, to which were added new letters, written specially for the book, and a section on the antiquities of the area.

The manuscript is an almost complete draft of the natural history (four letters are missing and two are incomplete), but with only a few leaves of the antiquities. Most of the manuscript is in White's hand although parts of it are written by others, almost certainly young relatives who helped copy the original letters which had been returned to him. While many of these have survived elsewhere two were incorporated here with the copies. The manuscript is not a fair copy, but a working document with many alterations which show how White developed the original material into the final text.

The White family owned the manuscript until April 1895 when it was sold to Sir Stuart M. Samuel MP. It was auctioned again in July 1907 and remained in private hands until 1923 when it was sold to Dr A.S.W. Rosenbach, the American bookseller, but it was not until 1940 that it was bought by Arthur A. Houghton Jr. When part of the Houghton Library was sold at Christie's in 1980 the Gilbert White Museum launched a campaign to purchase the manuscript for the nation and, accompanied by considerable publicity, it was bought for £100,000, of which the NHMF contributed £10,000. (This was the first occasion upon which the NHMF made a grant).

70 *A Cornfield by Moonlight with the Evening Star*
SAMUEL PALMER (1805–81)

c. 1830, watercolour with bodycolour, pen and sepia ink, varnished, 19.7 × 25.8 cm
The Trustees of the British Museum
1985-5-4-1
EXHIBITIONS: *British Landscape Watercolours 1600–1860*, British Museum, 1985 (ex-catalogue); *William Wordsworth and the Age of English Romanticism*, New York Public Library, 1987, no. 286

The fame of Samuel Palmer rests chiefly on a small group of works painted from around 1826 to 1832, when he was living in seclusion in the village of Shoreham in the Darent Valley,

Dear Sir,   Selborne: Aug: 1. 1771.

Letter 10:

From what follows it will appear that nei:
ther the owls nor cuckoos keep to one note. Well my friend
a friend
at Fyfield remarks that many (most) of his owls hoot
in B flat; but that one went almost half a note below
it. The pipe he tryed their notes by was a common
half-crown pitch-pipe, such as Masters use for tuning
of harpsichords: it was common London pitch.

A neighbour of mine, who is said to have a nice
ear, remarks that the owls about this village hoot in
three different keys, in G flat or F sharp, in B flat, & A
flat. He heard two hooting to each other the one in A
flat, & the other in B flat. Qu: do these different notes
proceed from different species, or only from various
Individuals? The same person finds upon trial
that the note of the cuckoo (of which we have but one
species) varies in different individuals: for about Sel:
borne wood he found they were mostly in D: he heard
two sing together, the one in D, the other in D ♯ who
                                                    sharp,
made a disagreeable concert: since he has heard one in
D ♯ & about Wolmere forest some in C. As to Night:
  sharp,
ingales, he says that their notes are so short, & their tran:
sitions so rapid, that he cannot well ascertain their
key. Perhaps in a cage & in a room their notes may
be more distinguishable. This person has tryed to
                            .... several other small

70

Kent, which he described as his 'Valley of Vision'. The drawings and paintings of this period are characterised by a combination of almost visionary exaltation and the close study of nature and rural life, which he invested with a spiritual quality. His flocks and sheaves of corn, his harvest moons and trees weighed down with blossom or fruit symbolise a passionate identification with a life of pastoral simplicity, inspired by his study of the Old Testament, Virgil and Milton. In time, his imagery became less intense, his style more conventional, as his youthful romanticism diminished, although a group of watercolours painted in the 1860s, again inspired by Milton and Virgil, recaptured something of the same mood.

This watercolour, one of the artist's undoubted masterpieces, belonged for many years to Kenneth Clark, and was well known in the circle of Neo-romantic artists who became famous in the 1930s and 1940s, including Graham Sutherland and John Piper, for whom Palmer was an important inspiration. Against an exquisitely rendered depiction of the Kentish landscape, the foreground figure with his staff and dog seems like a pilgrim about to enter Palmer's visionary world. 'Despite Nature's perfection,' Palmer had written in 1828, she 'does yet leave a space for the soul to climb over her steepest summits.'

Following the painting's sale in 1985, an Export Licence was suspended, and the British Museum launched a public appeal to raise the £200,000 needed. The NHMF provided a grant of £100,000, and other grants were from the Henry Moore Foundation, the Pilgrim Trust, the British Museum Society and members of the public.

71d (detail)

Common Buzzard by Charles Tunnicliffe, 1952.

71 *Charles Tunnicliffe Collection*

a) *Juvenile Greenland falcon*
   Watercolour, gouache, coloured chalks, pencil, pen
   and black ink on light grey paper, 59 × 46.9 cm
   inscribed with title and 'Jan. 11th. Length 23 in (585
   mm). Wing 415 mm. Weight 3½ lbs'
b) *Two green woodpeckers (female)*
   Watercolour, gouache, coloured chalks, pencil, pen
   and black ink on light grey paper, 46.9 × 59 cm
   inscribed '♀ Green Woodpecker. Obtained Malltraeth
   June 8th 64. Probably a first summer plumage because
   of the spotting on the flanks and underside. Wing
   163 mm. Bill to Tail 12¼ in. Green Woodpecker ♀
   Obtained from A.V. Crerden of Queen Elizabeth
   Grammer School, Bromyard, Hereford. Feb 7th
   1954. Wing 166 mm. Bill to Tail 13 in. Outer long tail
   feather. (This bird a victim of cold spell at the
   beginning of February)'.
c) *Fulmar petrel (suspected juvenile female)*
   Watercolour, gouache, black chalk, pencil, pen and
   black ink on grey paper, 65 × 49.8 cm, inscribed with
   title and 'Obtained from T.G. Walker, Henblas
   School by one of the scholars, who found this bird in a
   field near the school. Drawn Sept. 17th & 18th. Wing
   298 mm. Bill to Tail 17 in. Span approx. 40 in'.
d) Working sketchbook executed February–March 1951
e) Working sketchbook
   Anglesey Borough Council, Llangefni

Charles Tunnicliffe (1901–79) was one of the most gifted
wildlife artists of this century. Born in Cheshire he spent
much of his early life producing etchings and engravings
which reflected his rural farming background. Most of his
working career, however, was spent on the Isle of Anglesey
in North Wales where he found the inspiration for the vast
amount of illustrative work and major watercolours.

Elected to the Royal Academy, awarded the OBE, and the
Gold Medal of the RSPB, Tunnicliffe became a venerated
figure both in the art and ornithological world for the accu-
racy of his bird studies, the skill of his draughtsmanship and
composition, and his creativity as an artist. During his lifetime Tunnicliffe produced over 350 'bird maps' or detailed
measured drawings (mainly post-mortem) which were
drawn from life. These, in addition to over fifty detailed
sketch books, formed his basic reference material for finished
work and were greatly valued by him as the 'tools of my
trade'.

Upon Tunnicliffe's death Anglesey Borough Council was
able to purchase this Collection to preserve in its entirety.
They were given a £100,000 grant towards the purchase by
the NHMF and an interest-free loan of £50,000 to enable them
to rescue the Collection from public auction almost at the
eleventh hour.

The Landscape Park and Garden

CHRISTOPHER THACKER

'God *Almightie* first Planted a *Garden*', wrote Sir Francis Bacon in 1625. Without joining in theological dispute, we may agree that gardens have been cherished, admired, recorded in words and pictures, envied and enjoyed since earliest days. In astonishing contrast, however, is the general absence of concern about the collapse or disappearance of older gardens. With rare exceptions, it was not until the 1960s and 1970s that private or public concern at the destruction and irretrievable loss of these fragile, perishable creations became apparent.

Serious appreciation of historic gardens as a valid and valuable element of our cultural heritage began in the 1960s, and in the recognition of this the NHMF has played an important part. The decision of the NHMF to assist in the preservation and restoration of historic gardens runs parallel with the aims of the Garden History Society (founded in 1965), with the increasing participation of the National Trust in the care and preservation of gardens, and with the involvement of English Heritage (the Historic Buildings and Monuments Commission) since 1983 in producing the county registers of England's historic parks and gardens.

The parks and gardens so far helped by the Fund – and there will surely be more – already constitute a rich and inspiring group, characteristic of much that is most precious in this country. All are, in their distinctive ways, firmly 'historic', closely associated with the great course of British garden history. They range in date from the late seventeenth to the mid-nineteenth century, from the Chelsea Physic Garden, founded in 1673, and the formal gardens at Belton, to the varied aspects of the 'English landscape garden' represented by Studley Royal, Painshill, Kedleston and Sheringham, and to the Victorian marvels of Biddulph Grange. From the earliest to the latest, all have developed – and changed – since their foundation, some in their characteristics, some in their quality. Different problems arise in their use, preservation and restoration: the Chelsea Physic Garden is a 'working' garden, used for continuing botanical research; others form but a part of a great estate; Painshill was until the 1980s virtually derelict; and the garden of Biddulph Grange has suffered grievously from vandalism over the last decade. All are important, forming a vital and admirable part of this country's heritage.

The decision of the NHMF to help these gardens has been a momentous one, giving hope that other fine, yet threatened gardens may be kept from decline or destruction.

74. Gothic Temple at Painshill Park.

PICTORES OPERIS,
Heinricus Füllmaurer. Albertus Meyer.

SCULPTOR
Vitus Rodolph. Speckle.

72a

72 Chelsea Physic Garden, London

Chelsea Physic Garden Trust

The Chelsea Physic Garden takes its place in a long line of distinguished gardens devoted to the study, collection and dissemination of plants. It has always been a *physic* garden, specifically devoted to the collection and study of plants which have medicinal value. It was founded in 1673 by the Worshipful Company of Apothecaries as a means of furthering medical science, then thought to depend on the extraction of proper physic, or medicine, from vegetable matter. They leased a 3½-acre plot, with a river frontage, which remained whole until 1874, when the completion of the Chelsea Embankment cut the Garden off from the Thames. The original layout was geometrical, divided by straight paths, with rectangular beds on each side. Some of these were 'teaching beds' (Latin, *pulvilli*) in which groups of related plants might be studied as they grew. Rare trees and shrubs have long been planted in the garden, providing a rich and mature accompaniment to the layout of beds. The original geometrical plan was modified in the 1890s.

In the eighteenth century the list of notable employees and associates was astonishing. In 1722 Sir Hans Sloane took over the freehold; his statue has stood in the Garden since 1748. In 1722 Sloane appointed Philip Miller (1691–1771) as curator. To Sir Joseph Banks is due the unobtrusive but unique rockery, the first artificial rock garden in Western Europe, made from some forty tons of lava, black basaltic rock, that Banks brought back from his voyage to Iceland in 1772, and rubble from the Tower of London.

After fluctuating fortunes in the nineteenth and twentieth centuries, the Garden's role was confirmed in the twentieth century as a centre for plant research, and for the annual supply of thousands of plant specimens to other teaching institutions. Following financial difficulties in recent years, a new body of trustees, the Chelsea Physic Garden Company, took over the administration of the Garden in 1982, and in 1983 the NHMF contributed £60,000 with a condition that members of the public should have more general access.

a) De Historia Stirpium
LEONHARD FUCHS

Basel, 1542

This herbal marks a watershed – away from the stylised, often inaccurately copied, woodcut illustrations of earlier works, forward to drawings from living material, intended to be so accurate that little additional textual description was necessary.

Recent research shows that this volume was almost certainly hand-coloured in the original workshop at time of publication in 1542. It was a gift to the Chelsea Physic Garden from Sir Hans Sloane, former student turned landlord and generous benefactor to the Garden.

b) The Gardeners Dictionary
PHILIP MILLER

8th edition, London, 1768

Arguably England's most influential horticultural and botanical book in the eighteenth century – in effect, the first 'encyclopaedia of gardening' – written by Philip Miller, Gardener at the Chelsea Physic Garden from 1722 to 1770, and first published in 1731.

This volume, the 8th edition, the last published in Miller's lifetime, is botanically the most important: in it, Miller finally adopted the 'binomial system', proposed by the Swedish naturalist Carl Linnaeus in 1753 (and the basis for today's scientific naming of all living organisms), and so this edition remains the 'authority' for many current plant names on the strength of his 1768 descriptions.

c) Botanical Magazine
VARIOUS PUBLISHERS

England, 1787–1983

William Curtis, Demonstrator of Plants (in effect, director) at the Chelsea Physic Garden from 1772 to 1777, began to publish his *Botanical Magazine* in 1787, to illustrate ornamental exotic plants newly introduced to cultivation;

73. Humphry Repton's *Red Book* with the flap open.

published ever since (though incorporated into *The Kew Magazine* from 1983), it remains one of today's major botanical reference works.

This illustration depicts the New Zealand 'Kowhai', *Sophora tetraptera*, collected during Curtis's voyage with Cook on *The Endeavour* by Joseph Banks, and first introduced to European cultivation via the Physic Garden in 1771.

d) *Index Horti Chelseiani* unpublished manuscript from the library of Chelsea Physic Garden

by STANESBY ALCHORNE

1772

This slender volume marks two watersheds: the adoption of the new (but here, *strictly*) 'binomial' system by its author, Stanesby Alchorne; and the forced retirement of Philip Miller in 1770.

As its Gardener from 1722, it was above all Miller who made the Chelsea Physic Garden the foremost botanic garden of his day. Increasingly infirm, he became 'frequently refractory' with Alchorne as this catalogue of the Garden's plant collection was being drawn up in 1770, and was eventually made to resign.

Today, it gives us an invaluable record not only of the plants then in the garden, but also of how they were planted.

73 *Sheringham Estate, Norfolk*

The National Trust

Humphry Repton (1752–1818) submitted his proposals for the refashioning of Sheringham Park to Abbot Upcher in 1812. Sadly, Upcher was not to see its completion but he could anticipate the resulting transformation by studying the Red Book, a type of prospectus invented by Repton to show clients their landscapes both before and after improvement by means of watercolours with hinged flaps. That most of Repton's other Red Books are half the size of the Sheringham volume indicates the importance which he attached to this commission; to use his own words: 'It is with peculiar satisfaction that I leave this Record, of such a Specimen of my Art, as I never before had an opportunity of displaying: and should these hints be honor'd by your approbation & adoption, this may be considered as my most favourite work.' The vigorously undulating landscape created by the debris of ice-age glaciers as they melted into the sea was deftly exploited by Repton who provided the occupants of the hall with a continuous panorama of rolling pasture fringed by woods. But the most dramatic view is the one which opens up for visitors as they emerge from the main drive through the woods to see the house – a comfortable Neo-classical villa designed by his son John – sheltered under a thickly wooded hill, set against a sparkling sea which in Repton's time was made more picturesque by the sails of the numerous vessels which plied their way along the east coast. The park is not

74. View towards the Gothic Temple.

large. It is a microcosm of the English informal landscape tradition in its most perfect form, a masterpiece in miniature.

The Sheringham Estate, 770 acres of park, woodland and coastline, was acquired by the National Trust in 1986 for permanent preservation, with the aid of substantial grants including £254,000 from the NHMF.

74 *Painshill Park, Surrey*

Painshill Park Trust

This landscape garden was created by Charles Hamilton (1704–86), who, as an amateur in the late 1730s, began from scratch with some 200 acres of poor, heathy ground, which he transformed into one of England's most famous landscape gardens. In 1748 Horace Walpole said that Hamilton had 'really made a fine place out of a most cursed hill'. Hamilton gardened there with dedication and with genius until 1773 when he had to sell up.

Hamilton's estate was on sloping ground, falling towards the winding course of the River Mole. By means of a water-wheel (made to his own design) he raised water from the river to fill a long, winding artificial lake, with islands, which ran the length of the garden. Round this lake, and on the upper slopes of the ground, he set an intriguing variety of buildings: bridges, temples, both classical and gothic, a rough hermitage (with, briefly, a resident hermit), a ruined abbey, a medieval

tower or belvedere, a Roman mausoleum, a 'Turkish tent', and the most exciting grottoes of the mid-eighteenth century. Round these buildings, to separate them, and to allow enchanting 'prospects', were plantations of trees and shrubs, in which Hamilton made adventurous use of newly-introduced species (mainly from America); on one side of the lake was a vineyard, producing grapes from which, in favourable years, a 'fine champaign' was made.

Painshill quickly became famous, and both while Hamilton lived there, and for the rest of the century, the visit was a 'must' for tourists eager to see the best in English gardens. But by the early 1800s decline set in, and Painshill entered a century of neglect. Unlike many such creations, it did not suffer violent change, but was simply abandoned to the hand of time. Trees grew, matured and died. The buildings decayed, and some of them collapsed. Yet Hamilton's creation was never deliberately altered.

Between 1974 and 1980 Elmbridge Borough Council acquired 158 acres of the Painshill Estate, with the aim of restoring the garden, and, in 1981, the Painshill Park Trust was formed.

The lake has now been dredged, the woodland surveyed and cleared, and the lawns resown. Replanting of ornamental woodland near the Gothic Temple, in harmony with Hamilton's original scheme, was undertaken in 1987. The main buildings, such as the Gothic Temple, the Gothic Tower, the Mausoleum, the Grotto and the Abbey, are now restored or

75. The Banqueting House; illustration in colour on p. 19.

under restoration. The NHMF has so far offered over £1.4 million towards a management plan, and towards continuing restoration work.

75 Studley Royal, Yorkshire

The National Trust

The creators of Studley Royal were John Aislabie (1670–1742) and his son William Aislabie (1700–81). The former had first 'gardened' extensively at Hall Barn in Buckinghamshire. Chancellor of the Exchequer from 1718 to 1721, he was disgraced, briefly imprisoned, and then withdrew from Hall Barn to his property in Yorkshire.

He had little involvement in Studley Royal until after 1716, when the house was burnt. He then began to rebuild, and by 1718 work was also begun on the 'canalising' of the River Skell. However, the gardens in their completed form, including the incomparable Moon Ponds and the series of cascades at each end of the canal, were not realised until 1728. The Moon Ponds, combining a geometric purity of line in the circular and crescent-shaped pools, set in a simple framework of lawn and embankment, and backed by the steeply rising wooded amphitheatre, are a late and unmatched flickering of genius in the formal mode. The Temple of Piety, the visual focus of the Moon Ponds, was not completed until 1748. The lower area, with Fishing Lodges, and several of the garden

buildings in different parts of the grounds – the Rotunda, the Octagon Tower, and the grotto and rustic bridge – were added by 1732. The Banqueting House was not completed until the early 1740s. The architect Colen Campbell worked for Aislabie both at Hall Barn and at Studley.

Aislabie's plans at Studley included classical and gothic buildings in the larger landscape, and the hoped-for acquisition of the majestic ruins of Fountains Abbey, half-a-mile north of the main garden. He died before this was possible, but in 1768 his son William Aislabie acquired the site of Fountains Abbey, and in his time the parkland was considerably extended. One vista stretched far outside the estate, aligned on Ripon Minster.

The house at Studley Royal was destroyed by fire in 1946, and the estate was bought by the West Riding Council in 1966, subsequently taken over by the North Yorkshire County Council. In 1983, following the decision of the North Yorkshire County Council to dispose of the Studley Royal estate, the NHMF gave £2 m to the National Trust towards the acquisition and future maintenance of the estate. In 1984 a further £470,000 was paid to the National Trust to cover their payments to the Historic Buildings and Monuments Commission, towards the cost of maintaining Fountains Abbey. The present estate covers 760 acres, of which 610 are open to the public.

76 *Biddulph Grange, Staffordshire*

The National Trust

The gardens at Biddulph are as quintessentially of the mid-nineteenth century as Painshill is of the mid-eighteenth. They were developed from *c.* 1842 by the owner, James Bateman (1811–97) and his wife Maria, assisted from 1849 by Edward William Cooke (1811–80). While Bateman and his wife were passionate horticulturists (Bateman was an expert on orchids), Cooke designed the garden buildings and rockwork features. Cooke was as many-sided as any Victorian: he is remembered as a marine painter (he was an RA), and as an eminent geologist (for which he was made an FRS), and his connection with Biddulph is related both to his interest in rock formations, and in the architectural aspects of garden design.

Biddulph's garden scheme is remarkable for its variety, recorded in the *Gardeners' Chronicle* in 1856 and 1863, and again in the detailed sale catalogue of 1871. The gardens covered 14 acres, within a 1,750-acre estate, including a 181-acre deer park. There was an orangery, a conservatory, a fernery, and formal Italian terraces which overlooked a lake, with shrubs and woodland beyond, and which were aligned to one side with the long Wellingtonia Avenue. Round the house were horticultural or botanic features, separated by barriers of rocks, dense trees and shrubs, and linked by tunnels, passage-ways and winding paths. There was a collection of Araucaria (monkey puzzle trees), a pinetum, lawns, parterres, a 'geometrical garden', a rhododendron ground, a rose garden, a 'dahlia vale', a bowling green, a quoit ground, and the 'stumpery' – 'a picturesque assemblage of Old Roots, Rugged Stems, and Stumps of Trees, in all their gnarled, contorted, and varied forms'. This dazzling variety was eclipsed by two further features: 'Egypt' and 'China'.

'Egypt', or the 'Egyptian Court', enclosed by towering, pyramidal hedges of clipped yew, is in appearance the entrance to a tomb, carved in a massive cliff. Sphinxes flank the tiny entrance, hinting of labyrinthine mysteries. Sarcophagi? Sacred crocodiles? The passage leads through the rock to an Egyptian idol, and then continues, emerging in a half-timbered cottage, looking out to the pinetum.

'China', the most secret part of the garden, covers almost 4 acres. Walled round by cyclopean rockwork, China is approached either by a grotto-cave, or by a mysterious winding path. Chinese buildings represent the elements of the Willow Pattern – bridge, temple, steps and so forth – and other Chinese themes – a dragon parterre, a joss-house, and the gilded figure of an ox. The encircling rockwork, dominated by a watch-tower, is called the 'Great Wall of China'. Within this enclosure Bateman eagerly planted Eastern species, including Robert Fortune's newly-imported discoveries from China.

Since the early 1920s, Biddulph Grange has been an orthopaedic hospital. The hospital authorities have maintained the gardens, but many of the shrubs and trees have become overgrown. In 1977 the gardens and adjacent parkland were declared a Conservation Area, and in 1986, it was announced that the local authority and the National Trust would acquire the estate, with the National Trust taking on responsibility for the gardens. The NHMF has made available £300,000 to the National Trust to assist them in the restoration programme.

76. 'Egypt' with stone sphinxes, obelisks and pyramid of yew;
opposite 'China': the Chinese Pavilion before restoration.

Music and Literature

BRIAN MORRIS

That a pair of offshore islands in Northern Europe should have played so great a part in world history is surprising; that they should have generated and fostered a tongue which is today probably the world's dominant language is even more remarkable; but that so small a geographical area should have produced the literature which, for more than ten centuries, has reigned supreme in poetry, prose and drama, is little short of miraculous. Yet it is so. From *Beowulf* through Chaucer, Shakespeare, Milton, Johnson, Blake, Wordsworth, Austen, Dickens, Scott, Tennyson, to the great writers of the twentieth century, Lawrence, Eliot, Yeats, Conrad, and the like, English literature has been the supreme expression of the word in the history of man. No other civilisation – not Greece, not Rome, not China – can match this achievement, and it forms a rich part of the inalienable inheritance which has come down to us, and which we hold in trust.

The visible remainders of this heritage are comparatively few and visually unimpressive. Some medieval manuscripts are great works of art in their own right, but the same cannot be said of the holograph of a poem by Keats. A lock of his hair, or the chair in which Hardy sat when writing his novels, are not, in themselves, powerfully nostalgesic or stimulating to the imagination. Yet these and similar relics of the mysterious activity of great creative genius may help to remind those who see them that this earth of majesty, this blessed plot, has bred over the centuries the greatest writers the world has yet seen.

Music, on the other hand, washes over state boundaries and provides an international language for artistic expression. Yet Britain's national musical heritage is scarcely less impressive than its achievements in the other arts. In the history of European music British composers have played a decisive and directive part. The achievements of the Elizabethan and Jacobean madrigalians are unrivalled even in Renaissance Italy; Purcell is now recognised as one of the world's great composers, and in the work of that adopted Englishman Georg Friedrich Handel we may admire not only one of the greatest composers of sacred music but also the major dramatist of the eighteenth-century stage. British composers from Purcell to the present have given to European music 'a local habitation and a name' since so much of their work has been rooted in native folk-music, what Shakespeare called the 'stretchèd metre of an antique song', and this is nowhere more evident than in the music of the great composers of the nineteenth and twentieth centuries – Elgar, Holst, Vaughan Williams and Britten. Wales, Scotland and Ireland have made notable contributions to Britain's musical heritage. Indeed, 'the isle is full of noises, Sounds and sweet airs, that give delight and hurt not'.

78a (

you been able to get any information ~~concerning~~ concerning the earlier
of Germany? I find in Monsieur Raimond's translation of Coxe's
~~travels~~ in Switzerland, that Mr Bodmer a German poet of Zurich had
~~printed~~ him with a volume of amorous verses of the poets of the
~~thirteenth~~ century. This work is extracted from a manuscript which
~~Henry~~ of France entrusted to the city of Zurich in the year
~~13—?~~ I will transcribe the sentence which follows "Il m'a encore
~~é~~ (that is Mr Bodmer) le recueil de ses tragedies historiques &
~~tiques~~, ouvrage aussi savant qu'interessant — If it had been son
~~eel~~ the meaning of this sentence would have been evident, but the
~~savant~~ seems to imply that it is a collection of which Mr Bo
~~is~~ only the editor; unless, being original tragedies they are ac
~~panied~~ with notes. As to your hexameters I need not say how
~~by~~ the sentiment affected me. I have not been sufficiently accus
~~to~~ the metre to ~~give~~ any opinion which can be depended up
~~thing~~ strikes me in common with the German ladies that the
last feet are what principally give the character of verse to
Hexameters — the sum of my feeling is that the two last are mo
a verse, & all the rest not so much. I mean to say ~~that~~ that the
~~d~~ be more of the sensation of metre in the whole of the vers
~~break~~ the monotony of the two last feet. The lines also are
~~sufficiently~~ run into each other, but that might be easily
~~did~~. You do not ~~say~~ how you liked the poem of Wieland w
had read. Let me know what you think of Wieland —
make no mention of Klopstock; — and what is the merit
Goëthe's new poem? — Dorothy has written the other side o
sheet while I have been out. She has transcribed a few
~~riptions~~ — you will read them at your leisure. She will copy
two or three little Rhyme poems which I hope will
~~use~~ you. As I have had no books I have been obliged to
~~write~~ in self-defence — I should have written five times as much
I have done but that I am prevented by an uneasyness ~~near~~
~~ach and side~~ work a ~~kind of~~ dull pain about my heart. I have
the word pain, but uneasiness & heat are words which more
~~adely~~ express my feeling. At all events it renders writing ~~un~~
~~sant~~ ~~to me~~. Reading is now become a kind of luxury to me. When
not read I am absolutely consumed by thinking & feeling & bodily
~~tions~~ of voice or of limbs the consequences of those feelings.
~~the last stanza~~ of this little poem you will consider the word
~~time~~ "as put in merely to fill up the measure but as synonim
~~sense~~ ∙ ∙

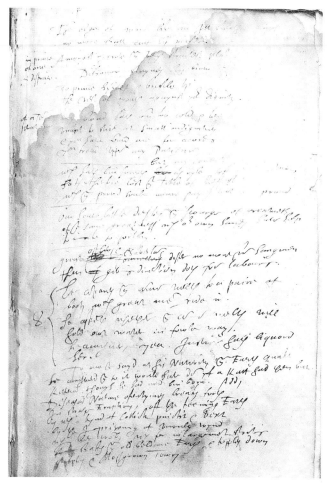

77

78d

77 Notebook incorporating contemporary extracts from Shakespeare's Henry IV, Part 1

ANONYMOUS

c. 1596–1603, 29.5 × 20 cm
The British Library
Additional MS. 64078

This anonymous notebook includes a personal selection of sixty-six lines taken from four out of the five acts of this most popular of all Shakespeare's English history plays. These appear to have been copied down not long after its first performance in 1596 or 1597, or at all events not later than 1603, and are the earliest commonplace extracts known to survive from any play written by Shakespeare or his contemporaries.

There remains an exciting possibility that these passages were copied from notes taken down actually in the playhouse. The fact that their arrangement faithfully follows the order of acts and scenes in the first printed text of February 1598 suggests that the copyist was working from the authorised version. However, variant readings of a kind evidently deriving from defective memory indicate that the immediate copy text was not the printed one. Sequentiality of extracts, coupled with garbled readings, apparently points to copying during an actual performance of the play, later supplemented by imperfect recollection. If this is indeed the case then the extracts would also stand as the earliest known instance of the contemporary practice, mentioned in *Hamlet*, of noting down passages heard during performance in 'table-books' or pocket notebooks.

The extracts are jotted on the flyleaves of a manuscript that also includes, copied in the same hand, a series of heterodox theological and metaphysical notes in Latin. A contemporary annotator has tentatively ascribed these to Thomas Harriot (1560–1621), the mathematician and scientist who was a friend and protégé of Sir Walter Raleigh.

The provenance of the manuscript is unknown. It first came to light at Sotheby's sale of 18 December 1986, when it was secured for the British Library at the hammer price of £165,000. The NHMF contributed £60,000 towards its purchase.

78 The Wordsworth Trust

The Wordsworth Trust, Dove Cottage, Grasmere

William Wordsworth (1770–1850) is one of the greatest of all the English poets. From 1799 to 1808 he lived with his sister Dorothy at Dove Cottage. It was here he wrote *Michael, Resolution and Independence, Ode: Intimations of Immortality* and completed *The Prelude* (1805). The daily life of the poet and his family is recorded in his sister Dorothy's famous Journals.

The Wordsworth Trust was founded in 1890 when Dove Cottage was purchased by a group of gentlemen to create a memorial to Wordsworth, not just for the nation, but for the eternal possession of 'all who love English poetry all over the world'. There are now over 80,000 visitors a year who come from 'all over the world' to visit the Cottage, the Wordsworth Museum and the Wordsworth Library, a centre for research into English Romanticism. The Trust has an educational role and has arranged a series of exhibitions at Grasmere, as well as an annual international conference on Romanticism. Grants now totalling over £100,000 have been made available to the Trust by the NHMF to help with the acquisition of important items for the collection and for vital conservation work.

a) The Goslar letter, written by William and Dorothy Wordsworth to Samuel Taylor Coleridge from Goslar, Germany, December 1798
EXHIBITIONS: *William Wordsworth and the Age of English Romanticism*, United States 1987–88

In the coldest of winters in a foreign city, Wordsworth's mind returned to crucial moments of his boyhood in the English Lake District. The passages of blank verse became seminal points in his great autobiographical poem, *The Prelude*, and include his account of stealing the boat on Ullswater and of skating on Esthwaite.

b) The restoration of Manuscript D of *The Prelude* exemplifies the ingenuity and fineness of Sidney Morris Cockerell's work who, until his death last year, had supervised the conservation programme for the Wordsworth Trust for almost twenty years. Manuscript D is open to show how Wordsworth has revised the text from the original drafts in the Goslar letter. Wordsworth was in the habit of pasting down sheets with wax and Cockerell devised a method of releasing the wax to show the manuscript beneath.

78a

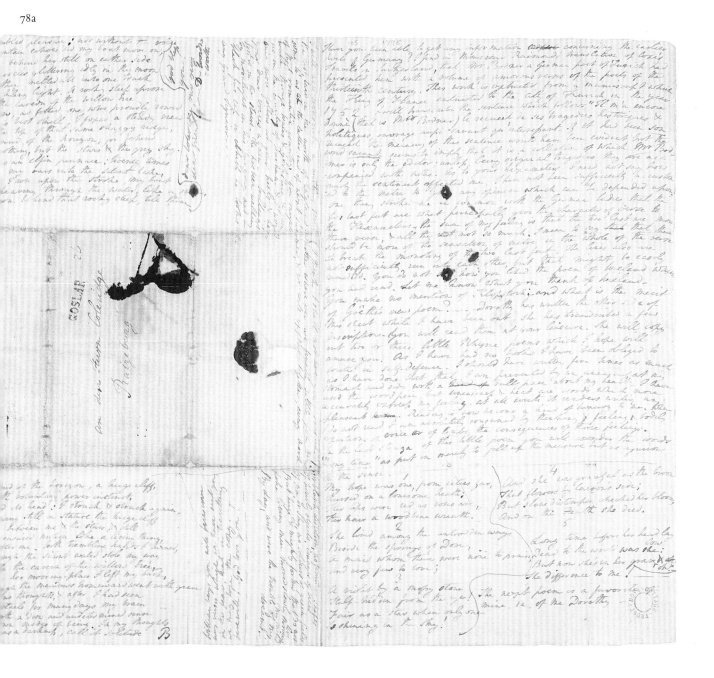

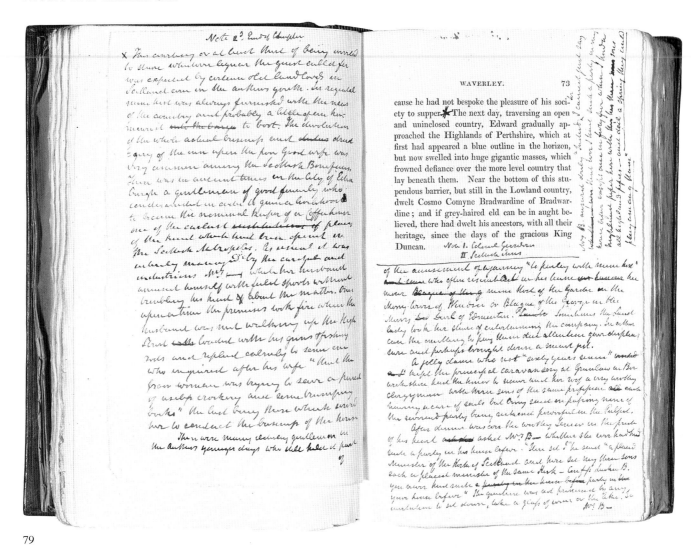

79

c) Portrait of *William Wordsworth* by Edward Nash
   c. 1818, pencil, 23.5 × 17.1 cm
   On the reverse is the inscription 'Wordsworth drawn for Southey by Nash'. Acquired by the Trust in 1981, an item among 2,000 letters and portraits from the estate of Raisley Moorsom.

d) Portrait of *Samuel Taylor Coleridge* by George Dance
   1804, pencil, 19.7 × 16 cm
   exhibited: *William Wordsworth and the Age of English Romanticism*, United States 1987–88
   Signed and dated 'Geo. Dance/March 21st. 1804', and presumably commissioned by Sir George Beaumont. It was drawn in London when Coleridge was waiting to sail to the Mediterranean in search of a warmer climate and better health. It was feared he might die abroad, and the portrait shows the wish of his friend and admirer to preserve his likeness.

79 *Waverley* and *Rob Roy* from the interleaved set of the Waverley Novels, known as the 'Magnum Opus'
SIR WALTER SCOTT (1771–1832)

Compiled 1826–32, 23 × 34 cm
The Trustees of the National Library of Scotland
MSS 23001 and 23006

When Sir Walter Scott went bankrupt in 1826 his immediate wish was to redeem his fortune and pay his creditors. A complete edition of his prose works, accompanied by introductions, annotations and corrections, seemed a way of doing this, and to help Scott with his task, he was given a set of his works interleaved with blank pages on which such alterations could be set down.

The forty-one volumes into which the set was bound, commonly known as the 'Magnum Opus', contain many thousands of corrections, and some 1,100 pages of additional text. The results were the first cheap edition of any author's works to be produced during his lifetime, and the re-establishment of Scott's fortune, but the effort of the work, so apparent on every page, drove him to his grave. The 'Magnum Opus' is one of the most remarkable association copies in all literature.

The set belonged to Robert Cadell, Scott's publisher. On Cadell's death it was acquired by A & C Black, who sold it in about 1930 to Temple Scott, a New York man of letters, from whom it passed to the bookseller James F. Drake. It then disappeared, and its whereabouts was unknown until it re-emerged in the library of Miss Doris Benz which came up for sale in New York in 1984. It was then offered to the National Library of Scotland by private treaty sale. At almost the same time the Library was offered the Scott manuscripts from the Pforzheimer Collection (including amongst other items *Quentin Durward*, and *The Fair Maid of Perth*). To take advantage of these two astonishing opportunities, the Library had to find $920,000. Without the NHMF's contribution of £325,000, these great purchases would have been impossible.

80 *Portrait Miniature of the 6th Lord Byron (1788–1824)*

ARTIST UNKNOWN

c. 1805, 7.4 × 6 cm
City of Nottingham Museums, Newstead Abbey

This portrait is believed to have been painted when Byron was a youth of seventeen, in the year when he left Harrow School and entered Trinity College, Cambridge. The verso bears an inscription in the handwriting of Byron's half-sister Augusta Leigh: 'This miniature of my "poor" brother was the best taken and given to me on my birthday'.

The portrait was first published by Doris Langley Moore in her biography *Ada, Countess of Lovelace*, London, John Murray, 1977. Mrs Moore records that Augusta had received the miniature from Byron and that after his death she gave it to Lady Byron 'who mislaid it for some years but found it with great satisfaction while arranging some papers'. She wrote to her son-in-law calling it 'a portrait of Lord Byron which I valued more than any other possession and believed to have been stolen. It was done at seventeen and has none of the misanthropic expression of all later pictures'. (Lovelace Papers, 15 October 1843).

The miniature passed from Lady Byron to her son-in-law Lord Lovelace, then to his son by his second marriage. There is evidence that by 1899 the portrait had left the family and entered the collection of Alfred Morrison.

Byron had inherited Newstead in 1798 when he was ten years old. By the time this portrait was painted he had already written several poems on the theme of his romantic ancestral home. The portrait was purchased for Newstead Abbey in June 1987 at the cost of £45,000 with funding from a number of public and private sources. The NHMF stepped in to provide the shortfall of nearly £8,000.

80

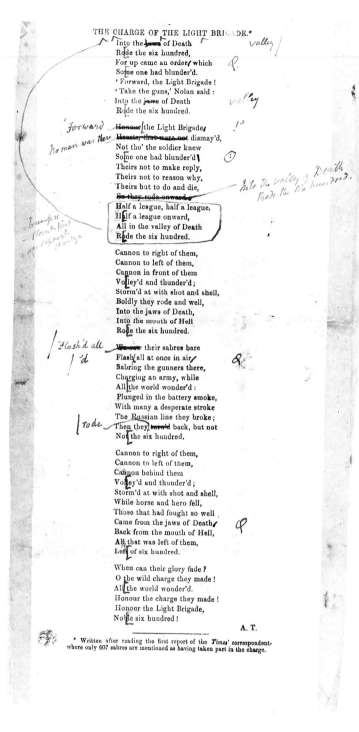

81b

Tennyson's reputation as one of the most eminent and influential figures of the Victorian era.

The Tennyson Research Centre, which is probably the most significant single collection of Tennyson material in the world, was established in the Central Library, Lincoln, in 1964 following an initial deposit from the Tennyson family. In 1980 part of the collection became available for sale. Through a National Appeal, to which the NHMF contributed £50,700, many important items were secured for the Centre including *In Memoriam*. In 1983 Lincolnshire County Council (in whose ownership the collection now was) acquired the remainder by private treaty sale to which the NHMF made a contribution of £48,500.

a) Autograph manuscript of *In Memoriam*
Tennyson began writing his masterpiece *In Memoriam* in 1833 following the death of Arthur Hallam, to whom the poem is dedicated. Within a few months of publication in 1850, some 60,000 copies had been sold. The Lincoln manuscript is the most complete autograph manuscript of the poem and is a comparatively late draft (the notebook being dated 3, 4 and 5 November 1842). The greater part of the poem is virtually a fair copy although the latter part of the manuscript is quite heavily revised and is thus more of a working copy. The Lincoln manuscript, together with the earlier less complete manuscript at Trinity College, Cambridge, are the two most significant manuscripts of the poem now in existence.

b) *The Charge of the Light Brigade*
After reading the account of the Battle of Balaclava, Tennyson wrote the first version of *The Charge of the Light Brigade* in one sitting. The first draft is in the hand of Emily Tennyson with alterations in Tennyson's own hand. The poem first appeared in *The Examiner* of 9 December 1854 after a number of significant alterations which can be seen in the first galley proof. *The Charge of the Light Brigade* became one of Tennyson's most popular poems. The poet had 1,000 copies privately printed, together with a message starting 'Brave soldiers . . .', which were sent to the troops at Sebastopol.

81 *Collection of Alfred, Lord Tennyson (1809–92)*

Lincolnshire County Council

In 1850, the most significant year of his life, Tennyson published *In Memoriam*, married Emily Sellwood and became Poet Laureate. The publication of further works such as *Maud*, *Idylls of the King* and *Enoch Arden* established

82 *The Revd John Chafy playing the Violoncello in a Landscape*

THOMAS GAINSBOROUGH (1727–88)

c. 1750–2, oil on canvas, 74.9 × 60.9 cm
The Trustees of the Tate Gallery, London
T 03895

The Reverend John Chafy (1719–82) was Curate of Great Bricett in Suffolk from 1749 to 1752, after which he moved on to wealthier livings in his native West Country. He is shown wearing a black suit and tricorn, seated on a grassy bank beside a tree, making music in a romantically fanciful landscape. Although to modern eyes he seems to be playing a viola-da-gamba, Chafy himself refers in his detailed will to 'the picture of myself playing the Violoncello, which was drawn by Gainsborough', and indeed it appears that until

83

about the 1750s this still relatively new instrument sometimes lacked a spike to rest on, being held between the knees like a bass viol. The pensive Arcadian atmosphere is enhanced by the presence of a stone urn and an architectural feature with a niche in which stands a figure holding a lyre, presumably emblematic of Music.

Gainsborough's most characteristic early works after his return to his native Suffolk in 1748 were small-scale full-lengths like this of local gentry posed informally in landscape settings of great poetic charm. Gainsborough was a keen musician himself and took particular delight in subjects of a musical bent.

The painting remained in the family until its recent sale, although it was for many years on loan to the Birmingham Art Gallery. Its sale at Sotheby's in July 1984 was seen by the Tate as a rare opportunity to acquire an important Suffolk period work by Gainsborough of a kind not yet represented in the collection. The NHMF grant of £50,000 was the largest of several generous contributions that enabled the Gallery to secure the work at auction for £100,350.

83 *Viol*

BARAK NORMAN (*c.* 1670–*c.* 1740).

London, 1713, label reading 'Barak Norman/at the Bass Violin/St Pauls Churchyd/London Fecit/1713', branded 'Barak/Norman/London/Fecit'
Horniman Museum, Inner London Education Authority
M 60-1983

The back of this viol is made from two pieces of maple, edged with a double row of purfling extended into arabesques at the bottom and shoulder; it is decorated with an elaborate, inlaid knot. The ribs are also of maple. The belly is of pine with double purfling, with single purfling surrounding the c-shaped soundholes. The inlaid design is hatched with *point d'aiguille* work. The head and pegs, neck, fingerboard and tailpiece are all modern reconstructions; the instrument had probably been adapted for use as a 'cello, a not uncommon fate for first-rate viols in the eighteenth and nineteenth centuries.

Little is known of Barak Norman's life. He was among the most highly regarded London viol-makers working at a time when English viols enjoyed a formidable reputation.

The viol comes from the collection of Arnold Dolmetsch (1858–1940), a pioneer in the revival of interest in early music and one of the first scholars and performers to recognise the importance of using authentic instruments and playing techniques. The Dolmetsch Collection consisted of three distinct sections which were acquired separately by the Horniman Museum between 1981 and 1983. The viol was part of the main section, consisting of eighty-five instruments owned (jointly) by Carl, Cécile and Nathalie Dolmetsch, which was bought in 1983 for a total cost of £121,130; the NHMF gave a grant of £30,724 towards the purchase.

84 *Autograph full score of Symphony no. 96 in D major, 'The Miracle'*

JOSEPH HAYDN (1732–1809)

24 × 29 cm, signed and dated '791 in London'
British Library
Additional MS. 64936, ff. 1v, 2

The violinist and impresario Johann Peter Salomon brought Haydn to London for two visits, each of about eighteen months, in 1791–2 and 1794–5. For each visit Haydn was to compose six new symphonies for Salomon's concerts. The twelve 'London' or 'Salomon' symphonies were the key to Haydn's immense success with the English concert-going public. Now known as symphonies nos 93–104, they were the last symphonic works he wrote and are the crown of his achievement in this genre.

Salomon was born in Bonn, settled in London in 1781, and, contributed to the capital's musical life up to his death in 1815. Haydn's visits were his greatest achievement and when Haydn left England, Salomon retained the autograph scores of symphonies nos 95 and 96. Sometime before the composer's final departure in August 1795, manuscript copies of the other ten symphonies were made, apparently directly from the autographs, to complete Salomon's set of scores of 'his' symphonies. These manuscripts were used in early

84

performances in England, and must have contributed to the published sets of parts issued in London by Robert Birchall some fifteen years or so after the works were written. Since that time they have acquired additional significance as the result of the loss of some of the remaining autograph scores which Haydn took with him on his return to Vienna.

From Salomon the manuscripts passed to his executor, William Ayrton, who, in about 1820, had them bound into four volumes, each of three symphonies. Ayrton frequently lent the scores for use in the concerts of the Philharmonic Society of London (of which both he and Salomon had been founder members in 1813), and, with a degree of reluctance, sold the whole set to the Society in 1847. In January 1988 the volumes were purchased from the Royal Philharmonic Society by the British Library for £600,000, to which sum the NHMF contributed £400,000. The Library was also assisted by contributions from the Baring Foundation, the Mercers Company, the Worshipful Company of Musicians, and others.

The Country House

BRIAN LANG

There is something quintessentially British about the country house. The house itself, together with its fine furniture, paintings and other objects, set in an extensive landscaped park, must be one of the more notable British gifts to civilisation. What is remarkable is that so many such houses, which were built mainly during periods of national economic prosperity, have survived so far into the twentieth century, with their contents and parkland virtually intact. Not that this has been easily achieved, and not without the destruction or dispersal of a very large number of houses and their contents. But compared to, say, France or Germany or Italy, the country house in Britain as a setting for a collection of beautiful things has enjoyed a conspicuous survival.

The role of the NHMF has been to provide the necessary resources to save the most important houses, and to find solutions for those in dire straits. This has been achieved in a variety of ways. What has sometimes been remarkable is the wave of public sentiment which has greeted the news that the contents of a country house face possible dispersal, resulting in the loss of the entity of the estate.

On 13 March 1984 the Chancellor of the Exchequer, in his budget statement in the House of Commons, announced that the NHMF was to be given an extra sum of money so that Calke Abbey, Derbyshire, could pass to the National Trust. This was the level of national interest in the future of this house, which scarcely anyone claimed was of top-ranking architectural importance. Nor were its contents thought to be of particular significance in themselves. The family associated with the house, the Harpur-Crewes, had played no great role in British history. The park at Calke Abbey was not a Stourhead, nor even a Biddulph Grange. But what almost everyone agreed on about Calke Abbey was that its whole was worth much more than the sum of its parts, because as an entity it expressed so vividly an eccentric strand in English country life.

But the National Trusts are usually organisations of last resort, when a family that has owned the house for generations is no longer able or willing to play an active role in the property. Where the family *does* wish to continue to participate in managing the ancestral house, the NHMF may be able to help achieve this. For Thirlestane Castle, Berwickshire, and Weston Park, Staffordshire, charitable trusts have been created, and their former owners help to manage the houses. The NHMF's role was in creating the new organisations which own the houses, and in providing the endowment funds for maintenance and upkeep, which cannot be met from revenue earnings of the property.

The NHMF is continually seeking new ways of finding solutions for country houses in Britain, and it is likely that each one saved through the Fund will require a specially-built mechanism, if additional responsibilities are not simply to be devolved to one of the National Trusts. It is highly likely, though, that as resources decline, decisions about which houses to save, and which should be left to the vagaries of other, possibly less permanent solutions, will become more and more difficult.

86

85

85 Thirlestane Castle, Berwickshire

Thirlestane Castle Trust

Thirlestane Castle, as it appears today, is the product of three periods of building, the 1590s, the 1670s and the early 1840s. The first, and only, Duke of Lauderdale, who was known as 'The Uncrowned King of Scotland', greatly extended and decorated the castle following his marriage to the Countess of Dysart in 1672. He also remodelled Ham House in Surrey, and much of the furniture from Thirlestane was eventually removed there. The immensely rich plasterwork of the State Rooms was begun by the English plasterer, George Dunsterfield, in 1674. He charged six shillings a yard for the more elaborate work and ten shillings a piece for the boldly modelled eagles and escutcheons on the main staircase.

The present owner, with the help of financial assistance from the Historic Buildings Council for Scotland, saved the castle from irreversible deterioration, but there were insufficient means to keep the building in a good state of repair. The NHMF helped to establish a charitable trust in 1983 to which the owner donated most of the house and its contents and some of the parkland. The NHMF donated a capital sum of £668,515 to the Trust to provide sufficient income to cover the cost of maintaining the house and opening it to the public. This procedure marked a new way of securing the future of an historic house in which a publicly funded body endowed a charity especially created for the purpose. It has come about through a partnership of private owner and the state, each of whom has made substantial contributions to the trust, and each of whom shares the common objective of seeing a great house properly cared for, and open to the general public.

86 Castle Coole, Northern Ireland

The National Trust
(See colour illustration on p. 119)

Castle Coole, the masterpiece of the architect James Wyatt, built between 1789 and 1795 for the 1st Earl of Belmore, has claims to be the finest Neo-classical house in Ireland. The masonry and carving of the Portland stone exterior and the precision of the joinery and plasterwork within are of the highest quality.

When Wyatt designed Castle Coole the standard method for fastening the ashlar cladding of Portland stone to itself and to the rubble structural wall behind was by means of iron cramps. Each block of the finely cut stone was in contact in at least four places with cramps which, over the intervening 180 years, had become damp and rusted. Rust causes iron to expand which in turn blows or breaks off the corner of the stone block. There was also the possibility of major structural damage occurring as moisture penetrated the building.

In 1980 the National Trust took the major decision to repair

87. The South-Front.

the damage being done by the cramps and decided to dismantle the exterior cladding of the entire building, section by section, to remove all the iron cramps, and then to rebuild the walls using stainless steel of the highest quality. As much of the original stone was reused as possible. The source of new stone was the quarry in Dorset from which the original stone was removed in 1790, thereby ensuring the closest possible match in colour and texture.

Whereas in 1791 some sixty-one stone masons, sawyers and cutters plus one hundred other workmen were employed using only hand-tools, in the 1980s the workforce consisted of a dozen men, using sophisticated modern power machinery and cutting saws.

When the stone cladding was removed a number of serious structural faults were discovered, especially rotting and potentially dangerous roof trusses, window heads and wall plates. It was a relatively simple matter to put these right once the covering wall was removed, and therefore a series of potentially expensive and disruptive repairs was undertaken as a part of the overall contract.

The stonework project was phased over a period of seven years at a total cost of approximately £3.2 m. The NHMF made a grant offer of £942,176 to the Trust towards the cost of this vital work. In 1983 the Fund also gave a grant of £246,000 to help the Trust acquire 345 acres of the parkland to protect the setting of Castle Coole.

87 Kedleston Hall, Derbyshire

The National Trust

Kedleston in Derbyshire has long been hailed as the early masterpiece of one of Britain's greatest architects, Robert Adam, and the epitome of English taste at the very moment Neo-classicism was beginning to overtake Palladianism as the dominant theme of country house architecture.

The Curzons, whose tombs fill the little parish church, have lived at Kedleston for over eight hundred years, and it was Nathaniel, 1st Lord Scarsdale, who began the reconstruction of the house after succeeding to the estate in 1758. Matthew Brettingham, James Paine and 'Athenian' Stuart all played a part in the early planning stages, but the young Robert Adam, recently returned from Italy, was put in sole charge by the summer of 1760.

Adam's revolutionary south front, based on the Arch of Constantine in Rome, marked a return to 'movement' in architecture, while his Marble Hall and Saloon (the latter based on the Pantheon) were inspired by the *atrium* and *vestibulum* of the ancient Roman villa. The architect's hand can be seen in almost every detail of the interior design and decoration, from the organ in the music room to the bookcases in the library, and the elaborate buffet display in the dining room alcove.

The house was meticulously restored by Marquess Curzon

of Kedleston, Viceroy of India in the early years of this century, but crippling capital taxes were levied after his death, and that of his nephew, the 2nd Viscount Scarsdale, in 1977. The present Lord Scarsdale's steadfast determination to secure the future of the house was finally achieved in 1987, when it was given to the National Trust. The family will continue to live in the east wing as tenants of the Trust, and thus the Curzons' 800-year-old links with Kedleston will not be broken. An unprecedented grant of £13.5 m was given by the NHMF, to provide an endowment and to acquire many of the contents. However, there is still an outstanding sum required to secure the future of Kedleston.

a) Sofa

JOHN LINNELL (1729–96)

c. 1762–5, gilt pinewood, upholstered in blue damask,
231.1 × 337.8 × 104 cm
Kedleston Hall
The National Trust
(Scarsdale Collection)
EXHIBITIONS: *Treasure Houses of Britain*, National Gallery of Art, Washington DC, 1985–6, no. 194

The idea of the four great sofas in the drawing room at Kedleston, with their triton, mermaid and dolphin supports, and their central medallions of Juno and Iris, Bacchus and Hercules, can be traced back to a design by Robert Adam, dated 1762, showing smaller and much more delicate caryatid figures. However, the London cabinet-maker John Linnell, who was entrusted with the commission, made important changes in execution, and the baroque character of the carving is reminiscent of his rejected design for George III's coronation coach of 1760, known from an engraving which

above 87b
left 87a (detail)
opposite The State Drawing Room with two Linnell sofas.

Linnell dedicated to the 1st Lord Scarsdale. The latter's interest in maritime affairs had earlier led him to consider a painted ceiling for the drawing room celebrating English victories over the French, to buy two large-scale models of warships which still exist at Kedleston, and to stage mock naval engagements on the lake below the house.

Samuel Wyatt, who was acting as clerk of works in August 1765, reported to his patron that 'the [first] sofa arrived safe, and it is certainly as elegant a piece of furniture as ever was made and as well executed. The gilding is by far the best done of any I ever saw, [and] it suits the place in point of size well'. The room still contains most of the Old Master paintings listed here at the same time, together with the original Exeter carpet and Waterford glass chandelier, a pair of pier glasses designed by Adam and a pair of inlaid card tables in the French taste, once again by Linnell. NHMF's grant has helped towards keeping this extraordinary decorative ensemble together in the house for which it was made.

b) Plate warmer
Design attributed to JAMES 'ATHENIAN' STUART (1713–88), made by DIEDERICH NICOLAUS ANDERSON (d. 1767)

1760, gunmetal and ormolu, on a mahogany parcel-gilt base, 114.3 × 52.5 cm, signed beneath the cover
'Diederich Nicolaus Anderson made this Plate-Warmer in the Year 1760'
Kedleston Hall
The National Trust
(Scarsdale Collection)
EXHIBITIONS: *Treasure Houses of Britain*, National Gallery of Art, Washington DC, 1985–6, no. 463

'Athenian' Stuart was consulted about the interiors of Kedleston before Robert Adam's arrival on the scene, and there is evidence that he sold Lord Scarsdale several Italian pictures still in the collection, as well as designing a huge two-storey dining room for the house in 1758. The drawings for this room show tripod perfume burners in the Grecian style, one of which still exists in the centre of Adam's dining room alcove, while a preliminary design for the plate warmer apparently in Stuart's hand also survives in the Kedleston archives. The metalworker, Diederich Anderson, probably an immigrant from Scandinavia who came to England at the invitation of Sir William Chambers, displayed 'a tripod, from an original design of Mr. Stuart's' at the Free Society of Artists in 1761, and may also have made a pair of bronze and ormolu chestnut vases which survive at Kedleston.

The plate warmer was made to stand in front of the fireplace, with its back open, and could have held a considerable stack of plates, compensating for the fact that the kitchen was in a separate wing, several hundred yards away from the dining room. The Duchess of Northumberland, who came here in 1766, described it as being 'in the shape of a vase and extremely handsome'. The pedestal was probably made to Adam's design by the carvers at the house, like the similar stand for the perfume burner.

'The Great parlour in the best taste of all' was how Horace Walpole saw the dining room in 1768, and apart from the loss of some of the gold and silver plate from Adam's buffet arrangement, it has been remarkably little changed since then. The magnificent plasterwork ceiling by Joseph Rose has inset paintings by Zucchi, Hamilton and Morland, while the pictures on the walls are also in fitted plasterwork frames, and have never been rearranged. The rest of the contents could easily have been dispersed with the enormous burden of capital taxes shouldered by the present Lord Scarsdale and his family. However, the rescue of the house, made possible by the NHMF, has ensured that such treasures are now more likely to remain *in situ*, where the public can best enjoy and appreciate them.

c) Nathaniel Curzon, 1st Lord Scarsdale, and his wife, Lady Caroline Colyear
NATHANIEL HONE (1717–84)

1761, oil on canvas, 265 × 183.25 cm
Kedleston Hall
The National Trust
(Scarsdale Collection)

Sir Nathaniel Curzon (1726–1804), 5th Baronet (raised to the peerage as Baron Scarsdale in 1761) was the creator of the house and park at Kedleston as we know them today. A keen amateur architect following the lead of his older friend and mentor Lord Leicester (the builder of Holkham), his purpose may well have been to create a Tory 'power house' in the county, which would rival the Whig citadel of Chatsworth. Curzon's marriage, to a daughter of the 2nd Earl of Portmore, had taken place in 1750, and 'Athenian' Stuart's preliminary design for a dining room at Kedleston, made about 1758, already shows a full-length portrait of the couple strolling in the park, hung in the alcove recess above the sideboard.

However, it was to be another three years before this project was realised, by the Irish-born artist Nathaniel Hone, and the picture was then placed above the chimneypiece in the state dressing room. Here it served as a culmination to the series of portraits hung throughout the three rooms of the state apartment, linking the Curzons with the Stuart kings. Despite its Neo-classical setting, in one of Adam's most ingeniously contrived spaces, the picture has a pierced gilt frame which is thoroughly Rococo in style. The informal pose of the young couple, recalling the pastoral scenes of Rococo painters like Hayman, also looks forward to later and more celebrated pictures such as Gainsborough's *Morning Walk* (Mr and Mrs William Hallett) in the National Gallery (*c.* 1785), or Romney's *Sir Christopher and Lady Sykes* at Sledmere (*c.* 1790).

The arch-enemy of Sir Joshua Reynolds, whose reputation later eclipsed his, Hone was nevertheless one of the most fashionable and sought-after portrait painters of his day. This work, which has claims to be his masterpiece, shows that he could be both innovative in composition and brilliant in technique. Thanks to the saving of Kedleston Hall by the NHMF, the picture will now remain in the setting for which it was specially painted, its sylvan landscape background reflecting the views of the park seen through the sash windows on the opposite wall.

88

88 *Weston Park, Shropshire*

The Weston Park Foundation

The present house was built to the designs of Lady Wilbraham in 1671 on the site of the original medieval manorhouse. In 1762 the estate passed to the Bridgeman family, who later became the Earls of Bradford. The house contains an important collection of pictures, tapestries and furniture. The park has a great number of ornamental buildings, among which is the important Temple of Diana by James Paine. The farm buildings have been described as 'one of the noblest architectural products of the agricultural "revolution" worked by the great landowners of the late eighteenth century'.

As an entity of house, contents and park, Weston Park is of considerable importance. When the late Earl of Bradford died in 1981 substantial tax liabilities arose and there was a danger that the house and contents might have to be sold. This danger was made even more acute as at the time there were insufficient funds in the government's 'acceptance in lieu of tax' budget to cope with such large liabilities.

The solution was found in the creation of a new charitable foundation, to which the house, park and the important contents were transferred. Much of this was purchased by the NHMF and then transferred to the charity, and the NHMF also provided a substantial endowment. This was partly made possible through the Government providing additional resources specifically to deal with Weston Park. The NHMF's financial assistance totalled over £7,700,000.

Sir Thomas Hanmer

SIR ANTHONY VAN DYCK (1599–1641)

c. 1637, oil on canvas, 110.5 × 88.3 cm
The Weston Park Foundation
EXHIBITIONS: *Treasure Houses of Britain*, National Gallery of Art, Washington DC, 1985–6, no. 63

Sir Thomas Hanmer (1612–78) was a page, and later Cupbearer, at the court of Charles I. A distinguished horticulturist and a collector of medals, he made a copy of Norgate's treatise on miniature painting and was the brother-in-law of Thomas Baker, subject of the famous bust by Bernini. Hanmer probably sat for Van Dyck around 1637. On Hanmer's death, the portrait passed into the collection of Lord Newport, where John Evelyn, who had known Hanmer well and had corresponded with him on gardening matters, saw on 14 January 1685: 'some excellent pictures, especially that of Sir Tho: Hanmers of V: Dyke, one of the best he ever painted.'

In its restrained colour and noble character this portrait illustrates Van Dyck's profound admiration for the work of the great Venetians, especially Titian. One of the most brilliant passages that Van Dyck ever painted was that comprising the bent wrist, gloves and shirt against the black of the costume. The form of the hand with the glove, the poise of the figure, and the glance help suggest momentarily arrested movement.

88. *Sir Thomas Hanmer* Sir Anthony van Dyck.

89 (detail). The State Bed.

89 *Calke Abbey, Derbyshire*

The National Trust

Until 1981 Calke Abbey in Derbyshire was probably the least-known country house of its size and importance in England. Generations of reclusive, and sometimes eccentric, Harpur-Crewe owners may not have welcomed visitors, but their retreat from the world meant that the house had been practically untouched since the middle of the nineteenth century. Not only the state rooms, shuttered and dust-sheeted, but also the rooms 'below stairs', the kitchen and laundry, the brewhouse, the blacksmith's and carpenter's shops, the stables and tack room, remained intact: a magical evocation of the past, and at the same time a wonderfully complete document of social history.

Calke never actually was an abbey, though it occupies the site of a small Augustinian priory, dissolved in 1538. The estate was acquired by Henry Harpur in 1621, but the present Baroque house was largely built by Sir John Harpur between 1701 and 1703, to the designs of an unknown architect, not the least of Calke's intriguing mysteries. The giant Ionic portico on the entrance front was added for Sir Henry Harpur by William Wilkins senior in 1790, and the exterior has remained little changed since that date – though much was done to the interior by Wilkins between 1792 and 1806 and by the Derby architect H.I. Stevens in 1842.

The consuming interest of the family through many generations has been in natural history and the sciences, more than in literature and the arts. A tidal wave of stuffed birds and animals, geological specimens and miscellaneous relics flows through many of the rooms. But treasures of other kinds abound too: an eighteenth-century print room entirely devoted to comic and satirical engravings; a drawing room still arranged exactly as it was in Victorian photographs, but with the brilliant colours of its textiles and wallpaper still intact thanks to the long-closed shutters; a Regency library hung with Ferneleys and other sporting pictures; and a huge wine-fountain by De Lamerie found at the back of a cupboard in the butler's pantry.

On the death of Mr Charles Harpur-Crewe in 1981, it seemed certain that the house would have to be sold to meet crippling capital taxes, its contents dispersed, and its magnificent parkland put to the plough (or, worse still, to the town planner). A vigorous campaign was mounted to prevent this, and the opening of the house for the first time to architectural historians and the press brought massive public support. But it was the initiative taken by the NHMF in bringing together the interests concerned, and producing a 'package', that was all-important. The reward came dramatically on 13 March 1984, when the Chancellor announced that he would provide the NHMF with a special grant of £4.5 m to save Calke Abbey: the first time that the claims of conservation and the heritage had been formally recognised in a budget speech. The house and park were acquired by the National Trust soon afterwards, and a three-year restoration programme was begun. Calke will be opened to the public on a regular basis in 1989, and Mr Henry Harpur-Crewe, whose personal determination to save the house counted for so much, will continue to have a flat there.

89. *left* the State Bed and *above* the front façade.

The Calke State Bed

English, early eighteenth century, with Chinese
hangings, embroidery of coloured silks and gold thread,
close-covered on oak and pine framework,
approximately 365.7 × 182.9 × 213.4 cm
Calke Abbey
The National Trust
(Harpur-Crewe Collection)
EXHIBITIONS: *Treasure Houses of Britain*, National Gallery
of Art, Washington DC, 1985–6, no. 375; on loan to the
De Witt-Wallace Museum, Colonial Williamsburg,
1986–7

The Calke State Bed, never before seen in public in this
country, is one of the most exciting country house discoveries
of recent years. Stephen Glover's *History of the County of
Derby*, published in 1829, provides a vital clue to its history:
'In this house, although it has never yet been put up, either for
use or ornament, is perhaps one of the most splendid state
beds in the kingdom, presented on the occasion of her marriage,
by "Caroline", Queen of George the Second, to Lady
Caroline Manners (afterwards Harpur) as one of her
bridesmaids.' Like so many stories based on oral tradition,
this is a muddled account that contains an essential element of
truth. Lady Caroline, a daughter of the 1st Duke of Rutland,
was not yet born at the time of Queen Caroline's marriage in
1705, but she is known to have been a bridesmaid to the
queen's daughter, Princess Anne, who married the Prince of
Orange in March 1734. Moreover, as her marriage to Sir
Henry Harpur took place in September of that same year,
only a short time after the departure of the royal couple to
Holland, it would have been very natural for such a gift to be
made as a 'perquisite' at that date.

The bed itself is likely to have been made about 1715,
perhaps for George I, although it has not been possible to
identify it with any certainty in the Lord Chamberlain's
accounts. The extraordinarily elaborate headcloth, with its
swags, gathers, pleats and ruched pelmet, looks back to the
engravings of Daniel Marot. But it is the brilliant colours of
the Chinese silk hangings, hardly ever exposed to the light of
day, which make the Calke bed unique. Most beds of this
period use contrasting materials for the inner and outer
hangings, and it is surprising to find the two mixed in this case
to achieve a particularly striking and exotic effect. The dark
blue is light in weight like taffeta, and densely embroidered
with flowers and birds, while the white is much heavier with a
satin finish, boldly decorated with processions of figures,
warriors on horseback, mandarins, and ladies in brightly
coloured robes, as well as dragons, birds, gazelles, and other
animals. The gold thread, which at first sight suggests a
later dating for the upholstery than for the bed frame, can be
found in documented early eighteenth-century examples in
Sweden, and a fascinating detail is the use of peacock feathers,
tightly rolled, for the knots of the tree trunks and the markings
of the butterflies' wings.

Whether because it was already considered old-fashioned,
or because Calke already had its full complement of four-posters,
the bed seems never to have been erected after its
arrival in the house in the 1730s. Indeed the timber
framework (apart from the close-covered elements) may
never have been brought up from London, since it would
have been cheaper for the estate carpenter to make a new one
than to pay the heavy cost of transport to Derbyshire. The
hangings appear to have been repacked in 1934 during the
time of the last baronet, Sir Vauncey Harpur-Crewe, and
some of the smaller pieces had notes attached to them suggesting
that they had been lent to an exhibition by his father,
Sir John. But otherwise they remained in store continuously
until the house was given to the National Trust in 1985, with
funds provided by the NHMF. A room is now being prepared
at the house, so that the bed can be seen in a carefully
controlled environment, ensuring its survival for many future
generations.

90

90 *A View of Verona from the Ponte Nuovo*

BERNARDO BELLOTTO (1720–80)

c. 1745–7, oil on canvas, 132.5 × 229.5 cm
Powis Castle (Powis Collection)
The National Trust
EXHIBITIONS: *Treasure Houses of Britain*, National Gallery
of Art, Washington DC, 1985–6, no. 193

Bellotto, who was Canaletto's nephew and trained under him
in Venice, lived in Verona for two years from 1745. This
painting shows the River Adige at Verona with Castel San
Pietro, the Visconti stronghold, in the centre background. It
was produced at the height of Bellotto's career, and is the
companion to another view of Verona, of which there is a
version on loan to the National Gallery of Scotland. Two
views of Verona were coincidentally sold at Christie's on 30
March 1771 as attributed to Canaletto, but for different prices
to that which the 1st Lord Clive (Clive of India) is recorded as
paying for the present picture (£147), also in 1771. It subsequently emerged that they were in fact copies by William
Marlow (see Horace Walpole's letter to Sir Horace Mann, 26
April 1771). One of these may have been the replica of the
Powis picture now in the Lee Collection in the Courtauld
Institute Galleries.

The present painting is first recorded as hanging in the
Dining Parlour of Clive's house in 45 Berkeley Square. It

probably entered the Powis Collection in 1784, when Lord
Clive's son married Lady Henrietta Herbert, who inherited
the Powis estates from her unmarried brother. Apart from a
brief period earlier this century when it was in the family's
London house, the painting has hung at Powis Castle since
the end of the eighteenth century.

In 1952 Powis was given to the National Trust, but this gift
excluded some of the contents. In 1981 the owners decided to
sell the Bellotto in order to meet capital tax debts and raise
funds, and it seemed as if the picture would almost certainly
be bought by a museum. The NHMF gave a grant of £160,000
to the National Trust towards its purchase, believing that it
should remain at Powis Castle, and that it was necessary to
avoid, where possible, a concentration of important paintings
in major cities.

91 *The Hill House, Helensburgh*

The National Trust for Scotland

In 1902 the publisher Walter Blackie purchased a plot of land
at the top of the hill in Helensburgh where his new house was
to be built. Blackie had been introduced to Charles Rennie
Mackintosh by Talwin Morris, the Art Director of Blackie's
firm and one of the leading designers of the new movement,
and persuaded Mackintosh to design the new house.

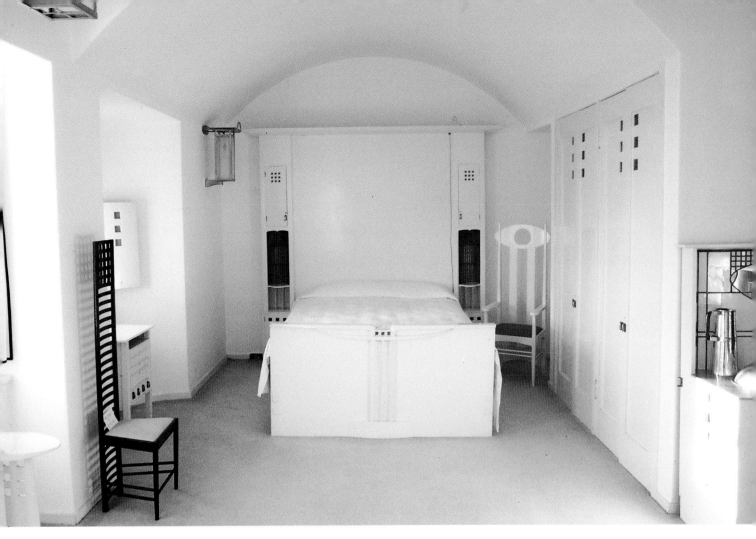

91

Mackintosh designed a twentieth century vernacular house, with a simple exterior, its impact coming from the contrast of flat expanses of harled masonry with the curves of the staircase and the bow windows. Mackintosh saw the house and each room in it as a unity, down to the smallest detail. His interior design would therefore include the shape and space of the room, the decoration of the walls, lights and light fittings, the furniture and the carpet. As Blackie noted, 'Every detail, inside as well as outside, received his careful, I may say loving attention: fireplaces, grates, fenders, fire irons; inside walls treated with a touch of stencilled ornament delightfully designed and properly placed'. One can see particularly Mackintosh's interest in patterns, from the geometric designs in the carpet and in the backs of the chairs to the curvilinear designs of flowers on the cupboards and stencilled on the walls.

The Hill House remained the home of the Blackie family until 1952. In 1980 the Royal Incorporation of Architects in Scotland, who had successfully preserved the house and contents, offered it to the National Trust for Scotland. The NHMF provided a grant of almost £500,000 to enable the Trust to preserve the house as a monument to Charles Rennie Mackintosh, as one of his finest designs.

Chair from the White Bedroom

ebonised oak, 140 × 40.5 × 33.5 cm
The Hill House, Helensburgh
The National Trust for Scotland

Only three items in the main bedroom were not painted white: the two chairs and the dressing-table stool. They are delicate and spidery and their black paint acts as a necessary foil to the expanses of white woodwork and furniture and the busy stencils on the walls.

92 *Nostell Priory, Yorkshire*

The National Trust

Nostell Priory in Yorkshire was begun about 1735 to designs by a local gentleman-architect, Colonel James Moyser, but executed (and modified) by the young James Paine for Sir Rowland Winn, 4th Baronet. The 5th Baronet (also Sir Rowland), who succeeded in 1765, commissioned Robert Adam to complete the interior of the house over the following decade in the newly fashionable Neo-classical style.

Almost all the furniture supplied in these years came from the workshops of Thomas Chippendale, and constitutes one of the chief glories of the house, together with Joseph Rose's plasterwork and Antonio Zucchi's decorative painting. When

Nostell Priory was given to the National Trust in 1953, however, the contents were specifically excluded, and capital taxes levied on the death of the late Lord St Oswald in 1984 meant that the family was forced to consider sales. The dispersal of such a collection would have been a tragedy, and the NHMF therefore offered to buy the major part of the contents of the show rooms at a cost of £6,102,160 to be given to the Trust.

Chippendale's commission to furnish Nostell gains enormous interest from the fact that he not only equipped the main rooms but provided items for the servants' quarters and domestic offices as well as supplying wallpapers, floor coverings and curtains. His authorship of over a hundred pieces and his frequently stormy relationship with Sir Rowland Winn is documented by thirty-eight letters together with various memoranda, estimates and a long series of bills spanning the years 1766–85. Several interiors such as the Library, the State Bed Room and the State Dressing Room still contain the full ensemble of furniture which Chippendale provided. The archive includes several fluent drawings sent by the cabinet-maker for his patron's approval which explodes the myth that he regularly made furniture according to Robert Adam's designs. Sir Rowland favoured richly styled but not ostentatiously splendid furniture, thus Chippendale's Nostell repertoire, while technically outstanding and made from superb-quality timber, displays a very English restraint. It possesses a special personality in the context of Chippendale's other work. The collection also includes important furniture designed by the architects James Paine and Robert Adam, as well as continental and Regency masterpieces.

a) Sir Rowland and Lady Winn
ARTIST UNKNOWN

c. 1770, oil of canvas, 104 × 126 cm
Nostell Priory
The National Trust
(St Oswald Collection)

This striking conversation-piece shows Sir Rowland Winn, 5th Baronet, and his Swiss wife, standing in their newly furnished library, the first room in the house to be remodelled by Robert Adam (in 1766–7), and still the most perfectly preserved of his interiors at Nostell. The famous Chippendale writing table (cat. no. 92b) is accurately depicted, but interestingly the artist has doubled the size of the room, portraying a range of two pedimented bookcases in the background whereas in reality there is only one. The interior is shown with Robert Adam's original light green, pink and white colour scheme, which was painted out by Thomas Ward in the 1820s with simulated maple-wood graining. The marble sculpture supported on a Neo-classical pedestal is a copy of the bust of the Medici Venus. This conversation-picture sums up the image of aristocratic culture and domestic happiness which English noblemen liked to project.

An inscription in ink on the back of the old canvas identified the sitters correctly, but ascribed the picture to Philippe Mercier, who had died about a decade before it could have been painted. Alternative attributions to Thomas Bardwell and Thomas Beach have been suggested, but the former

operated from Norwich and died in 1767, whilst the latter was essentially based in Bath. It seems most likely that this picture was painted locally – unless its inaccuracies indicate an artist working from drawings of the room and its furniture – but there is no obvious Yorkshire-based artist to whom it can be attributed. Since Sir Rowland's wife was Swiss there remains the intriguing possibility that the reason for the artist remaining unidentified in England is that he too was Swiss, possibly with a name similar to Mercier, or Le Mercier.

b) Library Writing Table
THOMAS CHIPPENDALE (1718–79)

1766, mahogany, the top covered with black leather, original gilt brass handles, 94.5 × 230 × 127 cm
Nostell Priory
The National Trust
(St Oswald Collection)

Chippendale's bill, dated 30 June 1767, reads 'To a large mahogany library table of very fine wood with doors on each side of the bottom part & drawers within on one side and partitions on the other, with terms of ditto carvd & ornamented with Lions heads & paws with carvd ovals in the pannels of the doors & the top covered with black leather & the whole compleatly finishd in the most elegant taste £72 10s'.

This table which combines magnificent richness and restraint is regarded as one of Chippendale's finest achievements. There is evidence in his earliest surviving letter to Sir Rowland Winn, dated 27 December 1766, that he felt particularly proud of this masterpiece and of a serpentine clothes press finished about the same time: 'Your honour thought it was best to send them by water on Account of the expence of land carriage. They are very good things and if the water should hurt them I should be very sorry . . . sometimes the damp of the ship affects the drawers and locks of good work which is made very close these are some of the best work that can be done.'

As supporting cast for the library table, Chippendale supplied six armchairs, an oblong stool incorporating folding steps, a drawing table, a medal cabinet and even sham books to line the doors. The whole repertoire survives in its original setting.

c) The Gentleman and Cabinet-Maker's Director, third edition, 1762
THOMAS CHIPPENDALE (1718–79)

Nostell Priory
The National Trust
(St Oswald Collection)

Thomas Chippendale was the first cabinet-maker to produce a lavish folio volume of designs comparable in importance to the pattern books issued by contemporary architects. The first edition, published by subscription in 1754, obviously helped to promote his trade because all known commissions date from after its appearance. There was a reprint in 1755 while a revised and enlarged third edition was published in

92

92b

weekly numbers between 1759 and 1762, the full set of parts making up a complete volume. A French translation appeared in 1763.

The third edition contains two hundred plates illustrating a wide range of fashionable household furniture; it was dedicated to HRH Prince William Henry, who later repaid the compliment by ordering furniture from the author. Chippendale's *Director* exerted a powerful influence on other furniture-makers, especially in the provinces; copies were also bought by members of the nobility who wished to keep abreast of genteel London taste. The acquisition of this volume may have induced Sir Rowland Winn to employ him to equip Nostell Priory, although it is more likely that Robert Adam recommended him as a cabinet-maker who could be trusted to design and make consistently distinguished furniture. Chippendale's home town of Otley lies only a few miles away, so (despite the lack of documentation) it is also possible that he was employed earlier at the house, by Sir Rowland's father.

d) *Armchair*
THOMAS CHIPPENDALE (1718–79)

1768, mahogany and beech, 115 × 72 × 59 cm
Nostell Priory
The National Trust
(St Oswald Collection)

Chippendale's bill, dated 22 January 1768, reads 'To 6 Mahogany Chairs with arms for the library the carving exceeding rich in the antique taste the seats covered with Green hair Cloth £36'. The frame (which has been French polished) illustrates Chippendale's transition from Rococo to Neo-classical ideals: the eloquent curvilinear backs are in contrast to the front legs and seat rails which betray the architectural heaviness of a table frame design. These stylistic problems had been resolved when Chippendale came to design a similar suite of armchairs for Lord Melbourne's library at Brocket Hall, Hertfordshire. The lyre design of the back splat was very appropriate for a library being the instrument of Apollo, God of the Arts.

The whole ensemble of furniture which Chippendale created for the Library at Nostell Priory survives, making it one of the most perfectly preserved of all Adam–Chippendale interiors.

e) *Barometer*
THOMAS CHIPPENDALE (1718–79 and
JUSTIN VULLIAMY (fl. 1730–90)

1769, tulipwood and ebony with carved and gilt ornaments, mechanism of polished and silvered brass and steel, 129.5 × 43 × 12 cm
Nostell Priory
The National Trust
(St Oswald Collection)
EXHIBITIONS: *Treasure Houses of Britain*, National Gallery of Art, Washington DC, 1985–6, no. 276

Chippendale's bill, dated 20 October 1769 reads 'To a very neat Case for a Barrometer made of fine tulip and other

woods & very rich carvd ornaments Gilt in Burnish Gold & plate Glass in the doors £25'. This is the only barometer (or clock for that matter) which Chippendale is ever known to have supplied, and it was specifically made for the Top Hall, where it has hung ever since. The instruments were made and charged for separately by Justin Vulliamy, a clock-maker with premises in Pall Mall who attracted Royal patronage. The magnificent case is by far the most richly styled object which Chippendale provided for Nostell Priory. His letters to a frequently irate Sir Rowland Winn chart the slow progress of work: the barometer took nearly eighteen months to complete and a further payment was made in November 1770 'To altering the ornaments of the Barometer frame and Gilding in Burnish Gold £1 3s' which shows that Sir Rowland, always a troublesome client, changed his mind about some decorative detail.

f) *The Nostell Dolls' House*
Attributed to THOMAS CHIPPENDALE
(1718–1779)

c. 1745, carcass of oak with marble chimneypieces and hearths; velvet, watered silk, painted chintz, and other textiles; walnut, mahogany, and ivory furniture; brass, steel, silver, porcelain, glass, and other ornaments; carved wood, wax, and composition dolls; 212 × 191.7 × 76.2 cm
Nostell Priory
The National Trust
(St Oswald Collection)

Family tradition at Nostell Priory has always maintained that the eighteenth-century dolls' house, one of the great treasures of the collection, was made by Thomas Chippendale. He made practically all the furniture supplied to Sir Rowland Winn, 5th Baronet, Robert Adam's patron, but he is also thought to have worked for the 4th Baronet, another Sir Rowland, before 1765.

Sir Rowland Winn's arms, impaling those of his wife, Susannah Henshaw (whom he married in 1729), are carved in the pediment of the dolls' house, but this is not to say that it definitely predates her death in 1742, for their children, Rowland, Edward and Anne, were then respectively three, two and under one year of age – hardly old enough to play with such an elaborate toy. Of course such a construction may have been intended for the amusement of adults as much as for children; but despite some old-fashioned features such as the panelling of the hall and parlour, the rectangular 'landskip glasses' above some of the chimneypieces, and the baroque form of the beds, a date of about 1745 is possible in terms of the textiles and costumes, and much of the furniture.

Whether the Nostell dolls' house is by Chippendale or not, it remains an astonishing feat of eighteenth-century craftsmanship: the microcosm of a whole country house complete with its furniture, textiles, silver, ceramics – and even its inhabitants, from the footman in the Winn livery waiting in the hall, and the chef in his starched hat in the kitchen, to the lady of the house in the state bedchamber, and a nursemaid with her charge in the chintz room on the floor above. Among the highlights are the longcase clock at the foot of the

93

93. *Colonel William Gordon* Pompeo Batoni

stairs, signed 'J^{no} Hallifax, Barnsley' (another reason for seeing the dolls' house as the work of native Yorkshire craftsmen rather than a firm of London cabinet-makers); the spit mechanism in the kitchen with an elaborate winding gear obviously made to turn; the drawing room on the first floor with cut-out French engravings, coloured to represent painted decoration; the three four-post bedsteads with their hangings respectively of crimson velvet, yellow watered silk and Indian chintz; and details like the marble chimneypieces, the tiny garnitures of *blanc-de-Chine*, the silver tea-table and the delicate ivory chairs. Perhaps the smallest object in the house is the glass mouse scurrying under the kitchen table, escaping from a dog with a rather mangy black velvet coat.

The only comparable dolls' house in England, that at Uppark, has been in the National Trust's guardianship for many years, so it is fitting that this other great family heirloom should have been saved for the nation in 1987 through the NHMF.

93 *Fyvie Castle, Aberdeenshire*

The National Trust for Scotland

The oldest part of Fyvie Castle dates from the thirteenth century. The five towers of the castle enshrine five centuries of Scottish history and each is reputed to have been built by one of the five families who once owned the castle. The building as a whole is possibly the grandest example of baronial architecture in Scotland. Behind its stout walls is its great wheel-stair – the finest in Scotland – and an interior that reflects the opulence of the Edwardian era. Portraits by Batoni, Raeburn, Ramsay, Gainsborough and Lawrence, fine furniture, arms, armour, and sixteenth-century tapestries make it one of the great treasure houses of the country.

Its purchase by the National Trust for Scotland in 1984 from Sir Andrew Forbes-Leith was the result of the Trust's swift and earnest campaign to save Fyvie from a fate worse than Mentmore. For not only is the house architecturally the most important of its kind, but it also contained the finest collection of portraits in private hands in Scotland. Sir Andrew's decision to put the whole castle on to the open market and its contents into the hands of Sotheby's caused a crisis in the Scottish heritage lobby. The successful outcome was made possible by the NHMF which provided the National Trust for Scotland with over £3m to purchase and endow the property.

Colonel William Gordon

POMPEO BATONI (1708–87)

1766, oil on canvas, 259 × 187.5 cm, signed and dated on block below column base at lower left
'POMPEIUS BATONI PINXIT / ROMAE ANNO 1766',
and by a later hand on architectural fragment at lower right 'Genl. The honble. John William Graham'
Fyvie Castle
(Forbes-Leith Collection)
The National Trust for Scotland
EXHIBITIONS: *Treasure Houses of Britain*, National Gallery of Art, Washington DC, 1985–6, no. 176

Batoni for some forty years made a speciality of painting British visitors in Rome. This is perhaps the most arresting of his Grand Tour portraits.

The sitter, William Gordon of Fyvie (1736–1816), was the second surviving son of the 2nd Earl of Aberdeen. Commissioned in the 11th Regiment of Dragoons in 1756, he became Lieutenant Colonel of the 105th Regiment of Foot in 1762, Colonel in 1777 and General in 1778. A close friend of the 4th Duke of Marlborough, Gordon was successively member of Parliament for Woodstock and for Heytesbury; from 1775 until 1812 he was Groom of the Bed Chamber.

This portrait was no doubt commissioned in emulation of Batoni's spectacular picture of Gordon's first cousin and nephew Alexander, 4th Duke of Gordon, painted in 1764, which is now at Goodwood. Batoni was also to paint a full-length of the Colonel's nephew Lord Haddo in 1775 (Haddo House, the National Trust for Scotland). The view of the Colosseum, the statue of Roma in the Palazzo dei Conservatori and the fragment of a frieze with a griffin appear in other portraits by Batoni. What gives the Fyvie picture so distinguished a place in the sequence of Batoni's full-lengths is the dramatic energy of the pose intended to set off Gordon's uniform, that of the 105th Regiment of Foot with the Huntly tartan. Batoni was accustomed to his patrons' vagaries of dress, but the plaid is unique in his *oeuvre*; James Boswell, a friend of the sitter, saw Batoni drawing Gordon's costume on 17 April 1765. The sitter was presumably aware of such portraits as Waitt's *Champion of the Laird of Grant* (Earl of Seafield), but in Batoni's hands the tartan is exploited in a classical guise.

The finest of the group of Gordon portraits at Fyvie, the picture was acquired with the latter in 1889 by Alexander Forbes-Leith, later Lord Leith, whose own acquisitions for the house reveal a particular penchant for military and naval portraiture.

Explorers and Travellers

ANN SAVOURS

It is difficult for us, living towards the end of the twentieth century, to envisage a world in which globes, maps and charts held many blank spaces. Yet at the beginning of this century, the continent of Antarctica had only been nibbled at, parts of the Sahara Desert and Central Asia were unknown and there was still speculation as to the existence in high northern latitudes of a great land mass or an open polar sea.

We should pause to think of our predecessors who sailed, steamed, walked and rode into those blank spaces and who abolished false lands of fable in earlier times. These islands have bred many explorers and navigators from the times of the Tudors. They ventured into the unknown for a multitude of reasons: out of curiosity, for the sake of adventure, for the sake of knowledge, for trade and colonisation, for spiritual enrichment, to gain worldly wealth, to spread the word of God, or as members of exploring expeditions, private or public, which sometimes combined the cause of geographical discovery with politics or science.

'What a vast amount of labour lies sunk in man's knowledge of the earth!', wrote one historian, Fridtjof Nansen, a great explorer himself in his *In Northern Mists*, London, 1911. The same writer emphasised the part played by myths and fables, which led men ever onwards (such was the *Terra Australis* of Cook's day). He also spoke of the spirit of man: 'knowing neither space nor time', some perhaps failed to find 'riches and favoured lands', but always returned with a greater knowledge of the world, so enlarging the spirit of the nation itself.

Capt. James Cook
of the Endeavour.

94 Captain James Cook, R.N.

WILLIAM HODGES (1744–97)

Oil on canvas, 76 × 63.5 cm
National Maritime Museum, London

William Hodges was trained as a landscape painter and his portraits are rare, but in this vibrant study he has successfully captured the strength of character as well as the rugged features of the great seaman.

Hodges was appointed by the Admiralty as the official artist to accompany Captain Cook on the second of his great voyages of discovery. The *Resolution* left England in 1772 and for the following three years Cook and his team of scientists and draughtsmen explored the Pacific. They charted its islands, collected plants, and travelled south into the polar regions searching for the mythical Southern Continent. During the course of the voyage Hodges produced a large number of oil sketches, and drawings, and on his return many of these were worked up into large canvases for display at the Royal Academy.

Unlike many of the landscape studies, the portrait of Cook was not painted during the voyage. Cook is shown wearing the uniform of a junior captain which suggests that the picture must have been painted in London in the period between Cook's return from the second voyage in August 1775 and his departure for the third and last voyage in July 1776. Cook held the rank of commander on the second voyage and was not promoted to captain until 9 August 1775.

Only three artists (Nathaniel Dance, John Webber and Hodges) painted Cook from life, so that this picture is of considerable importance and provides us with a new and striking image of one of the world's great explorers. Until discovered recently in an Irish country house the portrait was believed to be lost, and was only known through a somewhat idealised engraving by James Basire.

The portrait came up for sale and in 1987 NHMF offered a grant of £250,000 towards the purchase price of £630,000, thus ensuring that this important portrait remained in this country.

95 Cook's last letter to his patron

From the Cape of Good Hope, 26 November 1776
National Maritime Museum, London
AGC/C/15

The letter is addressed to John Montagu, 4th Earl of Sandwich and First Lord of the Admiralty.

The *Resolution* sailed from Plymouth on 12 July 1776, followed by the *Discovery*, Captain Charles Clerke, on 1 August. Cook reports on preparations at the Cape for the second part of the voyage. The Tahitian, Omai, had joined Cook in 1773 on his second voyage of exploration and after almost a year in England he was now returning to his native island. Cook describes Omai's pleasure at the sight of horses being loaded and continues: '. . . he has obtained during his stay in England a far greater knowledge of things than any one could expect or will perhaps believe. Since he has been with me I have not had the least reason to find fault with any part of his conduct and the people here are surprised at his

95 (above and below)

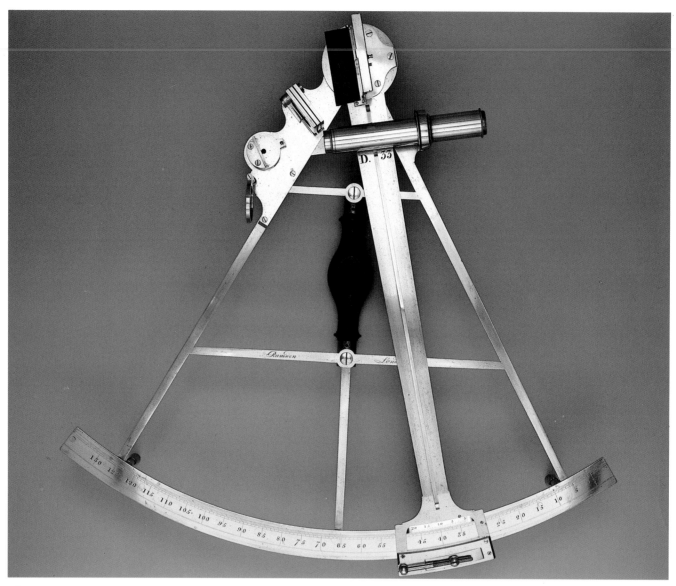

96

genteel behaviour and deportment.' He concludes with an assurance to Sandwich of his commitment and determination 'to accomplish the great object of the Voyage . . .'

The two ships sailed together from the Cape on 30 November.

This letter came up for auction in 1985, and the National Maritime Museum was very anxious to acquire it. The NHMF offered a grant of £8,793, being half the amount needed by the Museum.

96   Sextant

> c. 1770, signed 'Ramsden London', inscription 'D.33',
> radius 38 cm
> *National Maritime Museum, London*
> S 326

This sextant was used on Captain Cook's third voyage to the Pacific (1776–1780). It is one of only four known to have survived from Captain Cook's expeditions.

The sextant, one of the earliest used for finding a ship's position at sea, was made by the famous eighteenth-century instrument-maker Jesse Ramsden of London for the Board of Longitude. This instrument was provided for Cook's use by the Board of Longitude in discharge of their duty to 'make Nautical and Astronomical observations and perform other services tending to the improvement of Geography and Navigation'.

When the Board was dissolved in 1828 the sextant passed to the Admiralty Hydrographic Office, who had their inventory mark 'D.33' engraved upon it. The instrument now lacks its horizon mirror and the knob at the end of the tangent screw.

It passed through private hands and an institutional museum before disappearing for 40 years, only to reappear in 1982 in America. The sextant subsequently came up for sale in 1982, and the NHMF provided a grant of £6,500 to enable the National Maritime Museum to acquire it and return it to this country.

97 *Stanley Presentation Snuff Box*

1872, gold, decorated with enamel and set with
diamonds, height 3.7 cm, length 8 cm, width 6 cm
The National Museum of Wales, Cardiff
1986.20A
EXHIBITIONS: *Dr Livingstone, I presume?*, National
Museum of Wales, Cardiff, 15 November 1986–25
January 1987

The snuff box, which is of gold, decorated with enamels, and
with roses, thistles and shamrocks in diamonds, bears the
crowned cipher of Queen Victoria on the cover, and was
presented by the Queen to Henry Morton Stanley 'in recognition of the prudence and zeal displayed by him in opening
communication with Dr Livingstone, and thus relieving the
general anxiety felt in regard to the fate of that distinguished
traveller'.

In 1865 David Livingstone had journeyed into the interior
of present-day Tanzania. Four years later, after rumours of
his death reached the coast, the *New York Herald* dispatched
Stanley, one of their reporters, to find him. On 3 November
1871 Stanley was to deliver his famous greeting, 'Dr Livingstone, I presume' under a mango tree at Ujiji on the shores of
Lake Tanganyika.

Henry Stanley was completely unknown in London in
1871. Born in Denbigh in 1841 he had subsequently become
an adopted American. His exploit now brought him fame,
but in Britain he also had to face the criticism of those who
regarded his 'rescue' of their greatest explorer as a journalistic
stunt. One of his supporters was the editor of the *Daily
Telegraph* who tried to arrange a gesture of royal approval for
Stanley. He received this box, together with the Queen's
congratulations, on 17 August 1872.

It is clear from Stanley's journals that he treasured the box
for the rest of his life. In March 1986 it was sold by his heirs at
Christie's, and bought by an American collector. Its export
was delayed to give a British public collection the opportunity to match the purchase price of £106,200. This sum was
raised by the National Museum of Wales, with a contribution
from the NHMF of £41,000, in order to retain in the United
Kingdom an object so evocative of the great age of African
exploration.

97

98 *South Polar Diary*

LIEUTENANT HENRY ROBERTSON BOWERS
(1883–1912)

Scott Polar Research Institute, Cambridge

H.R. Bowers entered the Royal Navy as a cadet in 1897 and in 1905 was gazetted to the Royal India Marine Service. Ernest Shackleton's *Nimrod* expedition was in Antarctica at this time and Bowers followed its activities with much enthusiasm.

The culmination of his desires came in 1910 when, after a recommendation from Sir Clements Markham, Bowers was appointed to Captain Scott's second expedition aboard *Terra Nova*. The vessel sailed on 1 June 1910 with Bowers in charge of expeditionary stores. After a station was established on Ross Island Bowers was one of those in the depot-laying journey for the polar trek, and his navigation was of primary importance in this. He distinguished himself at the winter quarters, in particular during a difficult rescue as an iceberg broke loose, and on the winter journey to Cape Crozier. The South Pole journey began on 1 November 1911 and the last supporting party returned on 4 January 1912. Captain Scott, with Bowers, Evans, Oates and Wilson, reached the South Pole on 17 January 1912, thirty-three days after the arrival of the Norwegian expedition led by Roald Amundsen. Bowers had a small portable camera and a series of photographs of the site was taken. Much was against the return: weather, shortage of food, incipient scurvy, ice conditions. Evans and Oates died in the vicinity of the crevassed Beardmore Glacier. Finally, caught in a blizzard and only 12 miles from One Ton depot, the three survivors perished. The date 27 March 1912 is the last in Bowers' diary. He kept careful surveying records as well as a personal journal; the pages covering the polar journey provide a very close insight into the rigours and hardships that the expedition endured.

Bowers' papers, diaries and photographs came up for sale in 1985 and with a grant of £18,500 from the NHMF the Scott Polar Research Institute in Cambridge was able to acquire this historic record.

99 *Captain Oates's Polar Medal*

5th Royal Inniskilling Dragoon Guards Museum, Chester

Captain Lawrence (Titus) Oates was given special leave from his regiment, the 6th Inniskilling Dragoons, to join Captain Scott's 1910 British Antarctic Expedition. Only a few miles from the South Pole, the five men, Scott, Wilson, Oates, Bowers and Evans, realised that the Norwegian party, led by Amundsen, had reached the South Pole before them. Scott wrote in his diary: 'It is a terrible disappointment, . . . All the day-dreams must go; it will be a wearisome return . . .'

Ahead of them were the 900 miles of snow and hidden crevasses to base camp. Progress was slow, the weather deteriorated, with temperatures as low as minus 47 degrees, and the food supply grew short. They were not covering the distances they hoped to achieve. By that time the health of all five men was causing concern. Petty Officer Evans had fallen down a crevasse at the beginning of February, and had suffered severe concussion; he died soon after. Oates's feet had serious frostbite and he was scarcely able to walk. He was

99

very aware that he was holding up his three companions, and asked them to leave him behind. They refused. On the eve of Oates's birthday on 17 March 1912 Scott wrote in his diary: 'It was blowing a blizzard. He [Oates] said, "I am just going outside and may be some time". He went out into the blizzard and we have not seen him since . . . We knew that poor Oates was walking to his death, . . . we knew it was the act of a brave man and an English gentleman . . .'

Scott also wrote that 'Oates' last thoughts were of his Mother, but immediately before he took pride in thinking that his regiment would be pleased with the bold way in which he met his death . . .' When Oates's Polar Medal, which had been issued posthumously by the Government, came up for auction in 1984 the NHMF gave a grant of £1,000, which together with other generous donations enabled his regiment to purchase the medal and display it in their Museum at Chester.

100 *RRS Discovery*

length 52.4 m
displacement 1,620 tons
Maritime Trust

The Royal Research Ship *Discovery* was the last major wooden square-rigged vessel to be built in Britain. She was built at Dundee in 1901 for Captain Scott's first British National Antarctic Expedition (1901–04). Laboratories and a magnetic observatory were installed and her massively constructed hull could withstand being marooned in polar ice. Her significance is enhanced by her long and varied career: following Scott's first expedition she entered trade with the

100

101

Hudson's Bay Company; in 1925 she was rebuilt as an oceanographic survey ship and returned to the Southern Ocean for a distinguished series of expeditions.

In 1979, in urgent need of repair, *Discovery* was handed over to the Maritime Trust to be preserved for the nation. NHMF offered its first grant in 1981 and since then grants totalling £100,000 have been given to the Maritime Trust towards essential preservation work needed to save the ship from deterioration.

After drydocking at Sheerness and a thorough survey, a programme of repairs was put in hand. Areas of timber suffering from rot were treated. From March 1980 the work was carried out in St Katharine's Dock where the ship was on show to the public as part of the Trust's Historic Ship Collection. The ship's port side above the waterline was repaired while internal structural repairs continued, and compartments such as the galley, sick bay and laboratories were restored. The masts were refurbished and a new set of yards made, and the ship was rerigged as a barque for the first time since the 1930s.

In 1986 the *Discovery* was chartered to the Dundee Heritage Trust and returned to Dundee, where she had been built and where her restoration will be completed.

101 Film of the British Antarctic Expedition, 1910–13

National Film Archive

The Scott Expedition to the Antarctic of 1910–13 made an agreement with the Gaumont Company under which Herbert Ponting, expedition photographer, would make a film record of the entire trip.

Ponting had already made his name as a still photographer and had produced hundreds of stereo photographs for the Underwood and Underwood Travel Library. He took with him to the polar regions a wooden Prestwich camera, which is now in the Science Museum, London, and a specially-adapted Newman Sinclair No. 3.

On Ponting's return the film was edited and released under the title *The Underlying Story of Captain Scott*. A year later Ponting purchased the rights for £5,000 and presented, at London's Philharmonic Hall, a series of slides and film interlinked with his own experiences. It was the negative of this unedited film material which was recently preserved with the aid of a grant from the NHMF (cat no. 116). Ponting offered his services to the War Office but they considered his lectures themselves were an invaluable contribution to the war effort, so he continued to deliver them. Some of the film material was sent to the front line in France where it was shown to the troops, and by all accounts it proved a successful boost to their morale.

In 1917 Ponting decided to mount a second series of lectures at the Philharmonic Hall. They were not successful. He then arranged for the film material to be exhibited and shown under the title *The Great White Silence*. In 1933 a sound version was made and shown under the title *The Great White South*. This is the version you are seeing today.

Ponting's great skill was his ability to compose both still and film images. Considering the primitive nature of his equipment and the appalling problems of filming at temperatures many degrees below zero, the results are remarkable even by today's standards.

102

102 *The Halt in the Desert*
RICHARD DADD (1817–86)

c. 1845, watercolour and bodycolour, 37 × 70.7 cm, inscribed in the artist's hand on the verso: *'Ici on voit clair de lune peigné des recollections qui existent dans la tete du peinteur, et des certains marques et lines dans la livre petit que je crois de n'avoir pas ete dans la possession du Sir Thos Phillips. C'est sur le bord de la Mer Morte tout pres un petit rousseau entre le Jordan Fleuve et les Montagnes sur le route à St. Sabre.'* [sic]
The Trustees of the British Museum, London
1987-4-11-9

Richard Dadd was one of the most idiosyncratically talented nineteenth-century artists, known today mainly for paintings such as *The Fairy-Feller's Master Stroke* (1855–64), in the Tate Gallery, and for the fact that many of his finest works were painted after he murdered his father in a fit of insanity in 1843 and was committed to Bethlem Hospital (and later to Broadmoor) for life. This watercolour, probably painted in about 1845, was thought until its rediscovery in 1986 on the BBC programme *The Antiques Roadshow* to be lost. It is one of Dadd's most important early works and among the most impressive watercolours of the period.

In 1842 Dadd's patron, the lawyer Sir Thomas Phillips, took him as draughtsman on his expedition to Greece, Turkey, Palestine and Egypt; it was from this journey that Dadd returned insane. In November 1842 the party toured the Holy Land in exhausting conditions, described by Dadd in a letter to his fellow-artist William Powell Frith. In this watercolour, based on sketches made at the time, Dadd shows the party of European travellers bivouacked by the Dead Sea, where they waited for the moon to rise so that they might proceed by its light into the wild passes of Engaddi; Dadd himself is seated at the far right of the camp fire.

Untraced since it was included in the Great Exhibition of Art Treasures from the United Kingdom held in Manchester in 1857, this watercolour was described in the handbook as 'a most impressive "Moonlight Halt"', and as having 'all the solemnity which the blue sky, and broad pale moon, and twinkling white stars are calculated to impress on an excited brain, calming its horrors and lulling its rage to sleep'.

The watercolour was acquired by the British Museum in 1987 for a price of £99,700, half of which was contributed by the NHMF.

ANTIGUA

103a

103 *Columbine Collection*

CAPTAIN EDWARD HENRY COLUMBINE
(*c.* 1760–1811)

a) Views of English Harbour, Antigua, West Indies
b) Plan and views of the Island of Carriacou, West Indies
   Dated 1784 (Columbine's earliest known chart)
c) Cutter *Resolution* off Staffa, Scotland
National Maritime Museum, London

The Columbine Collection comprises sketches, charts, coastal views and ship-portraits, mostly finished in water-colour, by a naval officer, whose artistic and surveying talents extended well beyond hydrography.

Columbine's hydrographic interest was kindled in the West Indies between 1782 and 1790. When HMS *Sybil* was based at English Harbour, Antigua, he drew some fine views of the dockyard and the rest of Antigua. One chart of St John's Harbour, Antigua, was published by William Faden in 1793 but, like so many eighteenth-century surveys, few of Columbine's works saw publication.

From 1791 to 1796 he enjoyed command of the cutter *Resolution* off the west of Scotland. He cruised as far south as Cumberland and Northern Ireland, and north to Orkney and Norway, where he painted the castle at Bergen. His scholarly correspondence with the Society of Antiquaries of Scotland about the antiquities at Icolumkill (Iona) and the Orcadian standing stones is beautifully illustrated, and is interspersed with coastal surveys, views of castles and the basaltic formations of Staffa and Fair Head.

As Captain of HMS *Ulysses* in 1802 for a survey of Trinidad, he painted some of his finest views on the outward journey off Tenerife. After six weeks about his Trinidadian survey, he assisted in the successful capture of both St Lucia and Tobago before being assigned to the protection of shipping off Trinidad.

The Admiralty Hydrographic Office showed their esteem by appointing Columbine to the Admiralty Chart Committee in 1808. He was posted to Sierra Leone from 1808 to 1811, but his health deteriorated, and he died of dysentery on the passage home. Although he had completed few of his drawings, the Admiralty posthumously published his Sierra Leone survey and four other charts by him in 1816.

In August 1984 the two volumes of watercolours came up for sale. NHMF provided the total amount required to purchase the collection and its grant of £45,000 helped the National Maritime Museum save the Columbine Collection from dispersal.

104 *Sundial in tooled leather case*

HUMPHREY COLE (?1530–91)

c. 1568–9, silver, signed 'Humfray Colle'
The Trustees of the Science Museum, London

Humphrey Cole was the first native-born instrument-maker to practise a craft which had recently been introduced to England by Protestant refugees from the Low Countries. His work was held in high esteem by his contemporaries who described him as 'a very artificial workman' in the sense that

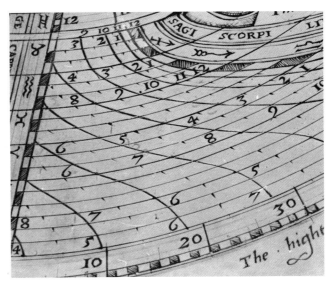

104 (detail)

he was extremely skilled in his art. Cole's work marks the beginning of the English trade in instrument-making in which England later became pre-eminent and his influence can be seen in the work of succeeding generations of instrument-makers.

This instrument is signed 'Humfray Colle' in a roundel that shows the planets which influence each hour of the day. Although it is not dated, Kathleen Higgins has been able to assign a date between 1568 and 1569 by comparing the signature with that on other dated Cole instruments. The upper surface has a sundial for use in a latitude 51°30′ (London) and a table in Latin based on the Greek doctrine of the four elementary qualities. The triangular-shaped gnomon of the sundial suggests that it is a conventional horizontal direction dial but the scale marked 'The heighte of the sonne' shows that it is an altitude dial of an unusual type. In order to read the time of day the instrument must first be positioned so that the shadow of the vertical edge of the gnomon lies parallel to the side of the horizontal plate. The inclined edge of the gnomon will then cast a shadow across the plate and the hour of the day is shown at the point where the shadow intersects the appropriate dateline. There are two sets of hour lines, one indicating conventional solar time and the other, marked 'The oures of the planets', giving the time in unequal hours. In this system of time measurement the period between sunrise and sunset is divided into twelve hours so that the length of the hour varies with the time of the year. On the evidence available at present this type of dial appears to be unique to Cole as the only other example is also signed by him. The underside of the square plate has a pair of sights along one side and a pivoted alidade whose position can be read on a quadrant scale. This enables the angles of objects above and below the horizon to be measured and by means of the shadow 'square' marked 'Latus Vmbra Versa' and 'Latus Vmbra Recta' the heights and depths of these objects can be found. Tables also give the position of twelve fixed stars and the date of the sun's entry into the signs of the zodiac. A figure gives the length of the sides of various polygons which would all fit into the same circle.

105b

The wooden case is covered with leather and decorated with various motifs including fleurs-de-lis and a Tudor rose.

This instrument is unusual in being made of silver rather than brass and it indicates the high social standing of the first owner. Apart from its function as a timepiece it is typical of the type of instrument which an Elizabethan nobleman would use to demonstrate his mastery of mathematics and astronomy.

The sundial came up for sale and was bought by the Science Museum with a grant of £20,000 from the NHMF.

105 The Searight Collection

The Trustees of the Victoria and Albert Museum, London

a) Janissary at the English Palace Constantinople

WILLIAM PAGE (1794–1872)

Watercolour over pencil on paper, 37.4 × 26.5 cm

Page, a British watercolour painter of landscapes and figures, travelled widely in Greece and Turkey after 1816. The Janissary portrayed here acted as a guard at the British Embassy.

b) East View of The Forts Jellali and Merani, Muscat

WILLIAM DANIELL RA (1769–1837)

1793, watercolour over pencil, 22.3 × 30.8 cm

The British landscape painter William Daniell assisted his uncle Thomas Daniell with drawings made during an extensive tour of India from 1786 to 1793. On their return to England they stopped off at Muscat where both artists made sketches of the harbour and later exhibited views of the subject at the Royal Academy.

c) Village Men Conversing with Two Armed Horsemen, in North Africa, possibly Morocco

ANDREW CARRICK GOW RA RI (1848–1920)

Water and bodycolour, on board, 35.7 × 51.7 cm

Gow was a painter of portraits, historical, military and genre subjects, and town views. He exhibited at the Royal Academy.

105a

105C

d) Derr

EDWARD LEAR (1812–1888)

1867, pen and brown ink over pencil, and watercolour, 34.4 × 50.5 cm, inscribed with title and date '4PM. 11 Feby 1867' and notes

Lear, famous for his nonsense rhymes and stories, was also one of the most intrepid nineteenth-century artist-travellers, travelling extensively to Europe, the Near East and India. In January and February 1867 Lear travelled up the Nile to the Second Cataract, visiting Derr on his return journey.

e) Ka'ah in the Harem of Sheykh Sadat, Cairo

FRANK DILLON RI (1823–1909)

c. 1875, gouache, on paper stretched round panel, 75 × 59.5 cm

Dillon was an oil and watercolour painter of landscapes and domestic Islamic architecture. In the 1870s he created an 'Arab studio' in his Kensington house with artefacts brought back from Cairo. The house depicted in this picture fell into decay at the end of the nineteenth century, but is now undergoing restoration.

The Near East and North Africa have long been a source of fascination to the West. Travellers have been drawn to the region by different interests, including commerce, politics, religion, classical antiquities, Islamic culture and mere curiosity. It was this variety of travellers' interests, as well as his own special interest in the subject resulting from many years living and working in Egypt, that enabled Rodney Searight to build up, over a period of twenty-five years from the 1960s, his unique collection of watercolours, drawings, prints and books.

The Collection now comprises several thousand items, dating mainly from the eighteenth and nineteenth centuries, the emphasis being on Turkey, Syria and Egypt, although less accessible areas such as the Caucasus and Arabia are also represented. Over five hundred artists and travellers are represented. They are mainly British, although there are contributions from French, Italian, German, Scandinavian, Swiss, Maltese, Eastern European, Russian and American artists as well. There are well-known names, such as Edward Lear and David Roberts, as well as a large number of lesser-known and amateur artists.

In 1985 the Collection was acquired by the Victoria and Albert Museum with donations from several organisations, including a grant of £20,000 from the NHMF.

Industrial Archaeology

DAVID SEKERS

The remains of the first industrial nation in the world are as significant as any other archaeological evidence from previous great civilisations. Since the Second World War industrial development has been destroying the traces of traditional industries, and some major landmarks were demolished in the 1950s and 1960s, including Wedgwood's Etruria Factory, built in 1769 and a monument to one of Britain's greatest eighteenth-century industrialists, and Euston Station with its famous arch, the symbol of Britain's pre-eminence worldwide in railway history. The aim of industrial archaeology is to record and preserve the key monuments of British industry. The extent of the work needed to be done was recognised when Ironbridge was selected as the site for the first International Congress on the Conservation of Industrial Monuments in 1973. Now most of Europe regards Britain as one of the leading nations to have recognised the historical value of its industrial past.

One form of preservation is through the creation of 'living' museums, a phenomenon in Britain of the last twenty-five years. Working machinery reveals the technical process and explains the functional nature of the building, and also emphasises the role of employees in the industrial setting. It is now widely recognised that the Industrial Revolution had a tangible impact on working lives and society as a whole, and is more than just a technological or economic phenomenon. Therefore, as at New Lanark, Styal or Coalbrookdale, the life of the whole community, as well as the works, has been considered an indispensable historical document. Bringing machinery back to life is not always easy and expert restoration work has to be carried out. However, it is seeing real machinery in a real setting with real skills employed that is the key to understanding industrial monuments.

The NHMF has recognised the importance of Britain's industrial heritage, and since 1980 has given various grants covering our textile, mining, shipbuilding and engineering past.

107

106

106   The Craigievar Express
Built by ANDREW LAWSON (1854–1938)

1895
The Grampian Transport Museum, Alford, Aberdeenshire

Postman Andrew Lawson built the *Craigievar Express*, a steam-powered tricycle-car, before the dawn of the motoring era in Scotland. Lawson was a keen amateur inventor and his imagination was captured by progress in horseless carriage design in Britain and on the Continent. His original intention was to build a steam carriage that would facilitate the delivery of mail in rural Aberdeenshire.

The vehicle is timber framed and composed largely of reused items of machinery. It features a small single cylinder steam engine, vertical boiler, two forward gears and a simple differential. Steering is effected by a linked lever and tiller device. Although capable of over 10 m.p.h. the *Express* must have found the appalling roads of the time hard going.

The Grampian Transport Museum, close by Craigievar (the birthplace of both inventor and vehicle), was keen to preserve and exhibit this remarkable machine in its original locality. In 1984 the *Express* was offered for sale to the Museum, at a favourable price, by its Surrey-based owner. The Grampian Transport Museum, a self-financing independent museum with charitable status, could not meet the purchase price unaided and launched a public fund-raising appeal.

Institutions and individuals had donated some £9,200 towards the purchase price of £15,000 as the deadline loomed large. The NHMF was approached and gave a grant of £5,800, thus enabling the Museum to make the purchase in 1985.

107   Big Pit coal-mine, South Wales

a) Lamps: Davy lamp, *c.* 1820 (replica); 'bonneted' Clanny lamp, *c.* 1860; Cambrian 'No. 1' lamp, *c.* 1930 (type still used today); and modern electric cap lamp
   Big Pit (Blaenafon) Trust
b) Smoke helmet: Siebe Gorman 'smoke helmet' used in rescue work underground; supplied with fresh air by foot-operated bellows, and with horn to signal to bellows operator
   Big Pit (Blaenafon) Trust
c) Wooden ironstone tram from the Rhymney area, dating from *c.* 1820, of a type generally used in the mines of north Monmouthshire, including, at one time, Big Pit.
   The National Museum of Wales

Britain's industrial supremacy in the nineteenth century was based on coal. By 1910 over one million men worked in the mining industry. The geography of the coalfields determined the location of the major industries and brought about great concentrations of population. For a century and a half geology essentially shaped Britain's economic geography, and the material evidence of the coal-mining industry is therefore an important part of our heritage.

Big Pit is located on the north-east rim of the South Wales coalfield, where both coal and ironstone are found near the surface and mining on a large scale began in the late eighteenth century, at first to supply the iron industry. Until around 1850 it was common for women and children to work underground as well as men, although this had been pro-

107a. Miners' lamps.

hibited in 1842. Women worked above ground at collieries well into the twentieth century.

The method of winning coal by hand changed little in 150 years. Today coal is cut by machine and transported by conveyors, but mechanisation is a relatively recent development. In 1913, the year in which the South Wales coalfield produced its greatest output, 99 per cent of that total was cut by hand. The coal faces at Big Pit therefore show the methods of hand-cut and semi-mechanised working which were typical through most of the life of the pit.

At its peak Big Pit employed 1,300 men. Virtually all the tools and most of the equipment they needed could be made and repaired in the blacksmith's shop and the fitting shop, both of which are now open to visitors. Other surface buildings open to the public include the winding engine-house and the pit-head baths, part of which has been converted into an historical exhibition.

The NHMF recognised the importance of preserving the colliery as a working museum, and have given several grants, totalling £30,000, to the Trust.

108 *Portrait of James Watt*
CARL FREDRIK VON BREDA (1759–1818)

1792, oil on canvas, 127 × 102 cm
The Trustees of the Science Museum, London

The partnership of the entrepreneur Matthew Boulton and the engineer James Watt in Birmingham from 1775 to 1800 was and has remained one of the most potent symbols of the

108

British contribution to industrialisation. Their products and projects wrought fundamental changes in British society, and were used and renowned across the world. By the 1790s the industrial and commercial successes of the Soho Manufactory in general, and of the separate condenser steam engine in particular were at their height.

This portrait is one of a pair, the other being a portrait of Matthew Boulton, painted by the Swedish portrait painter Carl Fredrik von Breda (1759–1818). It shows James Watt seated nearly full length towards the left, looking contemplatively beyond the table to his right on which lies a drawing of a rotative beam engine with condenser of the type produced in 1788 or later, with a wooden frame similar to that used by Rennie in 1792.

Breda was born in 1759 and studied at the Swedish Academy in Stockholm. In the years prior to his London visit, Breda had fulfilled several commissions to paint portraits of the Swedish royal family, and on his return to Stockholm in 1796 he became the court painter and leading Swedish portraitist.

During his time in London Breda worked in the studio of Reynolds and exhibited at the Royal Academy. He visited the sitters in Birmingham in 1792 with the engineer John Rennie, who had been in the employ of Watt from 1784 to 1791. In a letter to Rennie concerning the portrait, Watt wrote: 'I wish you to come this way when you set out on your journey and we can talk about the portrait to which I am rather averse as I think it an honour I do not merit and that my countenance cannot be worth procuring.'

In 1987 the two portraits came up for sale at auction. The portrait of James Watt was bought by the Science Museum for nearly £38,000 with a grant of £10,000 from the NHMF.

109 Matthew Boulton Archive
a) Design for minting machinery
Office of BOULTON AND WATT

No date, pen and ink, and watercolour 42 × 54.7 cm

While it is not known whether this highly complex design was ever executed, it represents the sophistication of the drawings produced by the partnership.

b) Design for the Imperial Mint, St Petersburg
WILLIAM HOLLINS (1763–1843)

c. 1800, pencil, pen and ink, and watercolour, 46.5 × 56.2 cm

Hollins had undertaken work for Boulton at the latter's house near Birmingham before being, it is presumed, involved with his Russian contract. Hollins declined, it is said, an offer to enter the imperial service as an architect.

c) Design for the British or New Mint
JAMES JOHNSON, AND OFFICE

1807, pencil, pen and ink, and watercolour, 41.3 × 66.4 cm

Boulton was engaged to provide machinery for the new mint on Little Tower Hill which was to be built to Johnson's design. The latter's death in 1807 led to the work being completed by Robert Smirke.

d) South elevation of Soho House, Handsworth
JAMES WYATT (1746–1813)

1796, pen and ink, and watercolour, 35 × 51.5 cm

This is one of a series of drawings for alterations to Boulton's house in Soho, Birmingham, produced in 1796. James Wyatt was perhaps the most celebrated of a family of architects and the designs for Boulton illustrate his taste for Neo-classical models much influenced by the Adams.

Archive Department, Birmingham Public Libraries

Matthew Boulton acquired an estate in Soho, Birmingham, in 1761 in order to build a factory for his silver and metalware manufacturing business. In 1766 he built Soho House as his own residence on a site adjacent to the Manufactory. Unfortunately, the original plans of the house have not survived. However, between 1787 and 1798 Boulton embarked on various schemes to extend his home and employed first Samuel Wyatt and then James Wyatt, as well as a local architect, William Hollins, on these projects. An extensive portfolio of drawings dating from this period was preserved by Boulton's family at its home at Great Tew, Oxfordshire. The portfolio includes proposed elevations of the house, ground plans, and at least one rejected scheme for a new house submitted by James Wyatt's pupil, John Rawstorne.

In addition to drawings and plans of Soho House, an important group of drawings relating to projects undertaken by Boulton and his partner James Watt has survived in this same collection. Plans of mint buildings and machinery in London, St Petersburg and Copenhagen complement the major business archive of this partnership donated to the Birmingham Reference Library early this century.

Birmingham Public Libraries purchased these drawings at auction for £48,480, of which £2,385 was provided by the NHMF.

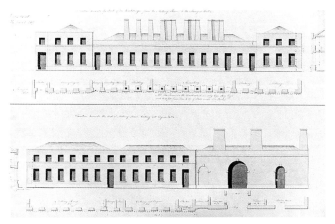

109c and *opposite* 110. Jacquard woven silk produced by Cartwright and Sheldon at Paradise Mill, Macclesfield, 1924.

110. Industrial village of New Lanark, Scotland.

110. Water wheel at Quarry Bank Mill.

110   *The Textile Industry*

The textile industry in Britain has long been accorded promi-
nence by historians of the Industrial Revolution. It was in the
cotton mills of the late eighteenth century that the age of the
factory began. The names of the great inventors and entre-
preneurs, such as Arkwright and Crompton, are justly celebrated, and the convulsive changes in working conditions
created by this revolutionary industry have been well recorded. It is fitting therefore that the NHMF should have been
instrumental in securing the preservation of key parts of this
story.

Arkwright personifies the entrepreneur who developed
and grasped the 'new technology'. The machinery which he
had patented by 1775 was the prototype of cotton manufacturing plant used throughout the world for the following two
hundred years. It is therefore of note that the Lancashire
County Museum Service has been able to secure a collection
of his earliest machinery, including a unique water frame.

The factory system was originally based on water-powered
cotton mills, and by the early nineteenth century had become
noted for the scale of employment, and the size of plant, as
well as notorious, in certain cases, for cruel working conditions. The regime of Robert Owen at New Lanark at this

time was a famous and spectacular experiment in enlightened
employment. The mills and factory village, which are being
successfully restored, are therefore a monument of international importance; the centrepiece of Robert Owen's work
there, the Institute for the Formation of Character, has been
restored with the assistance of the NHMF.

Another factory community of this period, noted for the
enlightened self-interest of the owners, was Styal, and here
the NHMF has contributed to the preservation of one of the
country's largest iron water-wheels, at Quarry Bank Mill.

It is probably no coincidence that the NHMF has recognised
that such relics are best presented in their relevant context: it
has assisted several important working museums that illustrate how widely dispersed the country's textile industry was.

The silk town of Macclesfield now retains a complete
Jacquard weaving shed, and the 1830 Silk Mill at Whitchurch
still produces silk, thanks to the NHMF. The Coldharbour Mill
at Uffculme illustrates the skills and processes of the West
Country woollen industry.

Textile industries have always been notoriously vulnerable
to economic cycles. One must hope that the same is not true
of museums, which now manage many of the key monuments of this industry. There is little doubt they would have
been lost but for the assistance of the NHMF.

110. The weaving shed at Quarry Bank Mill.

111. *The Maypole*; tiles produced by Carters of Poole in 1930 to decorate the Children's Ward of Middlesex Hospital, London.

111   *Ironbridge Gorge Museum Trust*

People come to Ironbridge to delight in the natural beauty of the gorge, and to marvel at the enterprise, the imagination and the achievements of those who lived here some two centuries ago during the Industrial Revolution. At Ironbridge the past is all-pervasive: bridges, furnaces, warehouses, inclined planes, mansions and cottages dominate the landscape. Even garden walls, constructed with kiln bricks, lumps of furnace slag, nodules of iron ore and discarded saggers are reminders that this was once one of the world's busiest workplaces, the scene of momentous innovations.

The Industrial Revolution could not have taken without cheap and plentiful iron. Yet before the Quaker ironmaster Abraham Darby I made the first usable iron with coke instead of charcoal at Coalbrookdale in 1709, eighteenth-century England, though a wealthy country, manufactured only a few pounds of iron per person per year. This great breakthrough by Abraham Darby led to many other important achievements: in 1720 the world's first iron wheels were cast in the Dale, followed three years later by the world's first iron steam engine cylinders. Iron rails were made first in the gorge in 1767, the first iron bridge in 1779, the first iron barge in 1787, and the world's first steam locomotive in 1802.

111. *Coalbrookdale, the ironmaking community, 1845.* Engraving by W.W. Law.

Not only coal and iron ore resources were exploited; the Ironbridge Gorge was also rich in clay deposits. As well as the many small-scale local brick and roofing tile manufacturers, there were producers of more decorative wares which were to attain international standing: the Coalport China Company made porcelain products while Maw and Company (established in 1852) and Craven Dunnill and Company (established in 1871) made decorative floor and wall tiles.

The NHMF has given substantial assistance to the Ironbridge Gorge Museum Trust with grants totalling over £285,000. It has helped to provide permanent protection for the Abraham Darby Furnace in Coalbrookdale, and, more recently, to acquire the remaining Coalbrookdale and Company Buildings, and to safeguard the future development of the Museum campus. The NHMF was also instrumental in the acquisition of some unusual items for the Museum's collections. The Deerhound Hall Table, designed by the sculptor John Bell (1811–95) and produced by the Coalbrookdale Company as its centrepiece for the 1855 *Exposition Universelle*, is the single most expensive item the Museum has purchased. Perhaps most unusual has been the support given to the Tile Conservation Team from Ironbridge for the rescue of Craven

Dunnill and Company's encaustic floor tiles from the Palace Chambers Buildings in Westminster, and, most recently, the two main wall panels from the Bernhard Baron Ward of the Middlesex Hospital.

112   ss *Great Britain*
Designed by I.K. BRUNEL (1806–59)

Bristol, 1839–43
ss *Great Britain Project*

ss *Great Britain* brought together steam screw propulsion and iron construction in the largest ship of her day. She was built to steam all the way on the Liverpool to New York run, but after grounding in Northern Ireland in 1846 she played a leading part in the emigration to Australia in the 1850s and 1860s, using steam as auxiliary to sail. She carried over 15,000 passengers to Australia between 1852 and 1876, with two breaks for trooping, to the Crimea in 1855–6 and to India in 1857–8. Finally she carried cargo, under sail only, to the west coast of America before being sold to the Falkland Islands Company as a store hulk in 1886. Despite being beached in

112

1937, she was salvaged in a dramatic operation in 1970, and returned to the Great Western Dock, where she was built, to be restored to the 1845 configuration seen in the model from Bristol City Museum.

Scrap wrought-iron arising from the restoration was given to the Ironbridge Foundry, whence it originally came, and the foundry has produced plaques commemorating the survival of the ss *Great Britain*, arguably the most important landmark in the transition from the square-rigged ship, which carried trade world-wide for three centuries, to modern shipping.

The chance ending of her working days in a spot so remote that there was no profit in scrapping her ensured her survival.

The ss *Great Britain* is now the centrepiece of Bristol's historic harbour, a massive artefact reminding us of the shipbuilders and seafarers to whom she meant so much. Restoration has been in progress since 1970, funded by donations and visitor revenue, and by two substantial grants from the NHMF totalling £50,000, the latest of which is for the building of a replacement skylight to cover the engine room, in which a replica of the 1845 engine is being assembled.

113. Photograph by Francis Frith, 1887 (see no. 114).

Movies, Piers and Postcards

C. CHAPMAN

The Bank Holiday Act of 1870 had a major impact on Victorian social life. Originally intended to benefit a specific group of working people, the Act secured a day-off in the summer for a large percentage of the population. Many factories were introducing half-day work on Saturdays and with most employers giving their workers a week off in the summer, the idea of the annual holiday soon developed. At the same time the railways were rapidly expanding and the new middle classes, representing the industrial and business prosperity of the country which had built the railways in the 1830s, began to exploit them for leisure activities.

The seaside holiday became popular as tiny fishing villages developed into coastal resorts. The attractions were endless. One could bathe, from changing-huts drawn by horses to the edge of the sea, or stroll along the promenade. There were entertainments on the sands; the Punch and Judy men, fortune tellers and donkey rides. By the end of the century a pier had become essential for any fashionable resort. The *Visitors Guide to Clevedon* of 1890 described its pier as 'a favourite promenade with visitors . . . they can derive all the salutary advantages of the pure sea air without any risk of the dreaded nausea so often induced by being tossed upon its wavey surface'. Over the years the piers were extended and adapted to suit the new generations of holidaymakers, and the 'What the Butler Saw' machines and pier theatres gradually made way for the amusement arcades.

The English seaside resorts reached the peak of their popularity between 1870 and 1914 and it was this period that the photographers captured so evocatively. The growth of a more prosperous middle class with an ability and a desire to travel ensured a ready market for topographical prints. Photographers would travel round the country with their cameras, and the result is a unique social record. Inspired by travelling showmen and tradesmen, the photographer Francis Frith set out to photograph every town and village in Victorian England. Frith's photographs cover every aspect of Victorian life, from the seaside piers, travelling fairgrounds and music halls to Queen Victoria's Diamond Jubilee.

The Jubilee procession of 1897 was captured on film and is a remarkable piece of early cinema. The first public display of cinematography was only two years before and from these early experiments cinema quickly evolved. The years 1895–1950 mark a great period of film-making. Early newsreels with evocative names such as Pathé and Movietone enabled cinema audiences to witness historic events as they had happened. Later came the feature films and the era of the great British studios.

This was a period of social revolution and much of what we associate with these times is now firmly regarded as part of our national heritage.

114

113 *Clevedon Pier, Avon*

Clevedon Pier Trust Limited

Clevedon Pier on the Bristol Channel is the most elegant of all
seaside piers, being notable for its high arched wrought-iron
spans, narrow promenade and delicate cast iron pavilions.
There are eight spans of 100 feet between the toll house and
the pier head. Built by Grover and Ward in 1869 with unused
'Barlow rails' designed by Isambard Brunel for his wide-
gauged railway, it represents an unusual and clever blend of
material and Victorian technology. Sir John Betjeman said of
the pier: 'It is, in itself, a beautiful and elegant pier. It recalls a
painting by Turner or an etching by Whistler or Sickert or
even a Japanese print. Without its pier, Clevedon would be a
diamond with a flaw.'

For about a hundred years seaside piers had periods of high
activity and Clevedon was no exception, especially in the
1950s and 1960s when a fleet of paddle steamers regularly
ploughed the waves of the Bristol Channel between South
Wales and Somerset, always calling at the pier. However, in
1970 two spans collapsed into the sea during insurance tests,
isolating the pier head from the promenade. There they
remained for over ten years in an era of high inflation and
public apathy towards conservation.

As a result of a public inquiry in 1980 when the owners

sought to demolish the Grade 11★ structure, a newly-formed
Clevedon Pier Trust was able to obtain a ninety-nine-year
lease of the Pier. With a viable engineering scheme for its
restoration, £500,000 was granted to the Trust by the NHMF
and a similar donation from English Heritage enabled work
to proceed. The Pier is now restored, having been dismantled
and transported to a land-based site, and the second phase of a
£1.8 m restoration programme is in hand for the return of the
main structure to Clevedon in the summer of 1988.

114 *Francis Frith photographic negative archive*

History and Geography Dept. Birmingham Public Libraries

The Francis Frith photographic negative archive is, perhaps,
the largest British collection of topographical views in existence and provides an unrivalled record of the way in which
the urban and rural scene in our country has changed in the
period between about 1870 and 1970.

The archive comprises 312,000 negatives on glass and
celluloid produced by the Francis Frith Company which was
founded at Reigate in 1860 and which continued to trade until
it went into liquidation in 1971. The very earliest negatives
produced by the founder, Francis Frith (1822–98), and in fact

the majority of those made prior to about 1870 have not survived but those that do exist provide us with a valuable record of the changes that have taken place in particular places since the company's photographers often revisited popular holiday resorts to up-date their views.

Francis Frith was born in 1822 at Chesterfield in Derbyshire into the family of a pious Quaker tradesman. Francis was the only son and at the age of twelve was sent off to the Quaker Camp Hill boarding school in Birmingham where he remained until 1838. Upon leaving school he was apprenticed, probably to a Sheffield Cutler, and remained in this employment until 1843 when he appears to have suffered a nervous breakdown.

His recovery was assisted by an extensive tour of Britain and it was during this convalescence that he not only discovered the beauty of his native land but also became acquainted with the new art of photography. Between 1845 and 1854 he was involved in a grocery business in Liverpool but his new interest was not neglected for in 1853 he became a founder member of the Liverpool Photographic Society. By 1856 he was exhibiting in London and in the following year he was undertaking the first of three expeditions to Egypt and the Holy Land. The publication of his labours generated much interest and he was soon hailed as one of the leading photographers of his day. While in the midst of all this work he married a Quaker girl from Reigate and it was there that he

established his photographic business, probably in 1860. The business flourished and was soon fulfilling the popular demand for photographs of holiday resorts and the towns, villages and beauty spots of the country which people were beginning to visit in ever growing numbers. The heyday of the company was between about 1890 and 1920 but the photographers were still active until the company ceased trading.

The acquisition of the Francis Frith photographic negative archive by Birmingham Public Libraries in 1985 was only made possible by most generous grants and donations from the NHMF and by other bodies and private individuals. NHMF provided a grant of £75,000.

115 Edwards's Gallopers
The Fairground Heritage Trust

At the end of the nineteenth century Britain led the world in the manufacture of fairground roundabouts. Of the great variety of amusement devices created, the most durable has been the steam-driven wooden horse roundabout, known as the Gallopers.

Following the introduction of faster electric roundabouts between the wars, Gallopers declined in popularity and their numbers dramatically decreased, while those that remained

115. The Gallopers in the 1920s.

115 (detail)

116. *Black Narcissus* directed by Michael Powell and Emeric Pressburger in 1947 with Jean Simmons.

116. Poster for the 1944 production of *Henry V*.

were invariably converted to electric drive. Thanks to a recent interest in steam preservation, these splendid old machines are being recognised as valuable relics of our social and industrial heritage.

The Edwards's Gallopers, an Edwardian steam-powered roundabout, boasts thirty-six wooden horses and cockerels, mostly the work of Britain's finest fairground carver, Arthur Anderson of Bristol. The Edwards family who travelled the roundabout carefully stored it away over half a century ago.

In 1986 the NHMF gave a grant of £22,000 to the newly formed Fairground Heritage Trust towards the purchase of the Gallopers, together with its Tidman steam centre engine, Verbeeck organ and 1917 FWD lorry and packing truck, for £57,000. Much of this is in the process of being restored.

116. Laurence Olivier in the title-role of *Henry V* directed by him in 1944.

116. *Blithe Spirit*; directed by David Lean in 1944 with Constance Cummings, Kay Hammond and Rex Harrison.

116. Production-still from *Blackmail*, 1929. Directed by Alfred Hitchcock (*centre*) with Anny Ondra.

116   *Film from the National Film Archive*

National Film Archive

It was in 1935 that the British Film Institute implemented the article in its Articles and Memorandum of Association which enabled it to establish a national repository of films of permanent value. However, much cinema history had already come and gone because nitrate film, the base material on which moving images were supported, is highly inflammable. Because of this, few film-makers, producers or distributors chose to retain films after their commercial life was over. Film on nitrate stock will also eventually decompose and the National Film Archive has been battling to preserve the films in its care. In 1980 the NHMF offered its first grant to the British Film Institute to transfer the film on to safety stock and thus halt decomposition.

As a result, some of the great feature films of British cinema, such as *Henry v*, *The Red Shoes*, *Black Narcissus* and *A Matter of Life and Death*, have been restored over the last two years. Similarly, British documentary films and newsreels are being copied before the images are destroyed.

The Archive also holds a comprehensive collection of black-and-white still photographs. These stills, many of which refer to films made by early British companies no longer in existence, are also deteriorating and the Archive, again with the help of the NHMF, is restoring them. The collection includes photographs from the Boer War (1899–1900), and First World War photographs taken in 1914 by Joseph Rosenthal while he was an official Canadian war photographer. Material from the great studios, London Film, Twickenham and Ealing, is also being restored.

Historians of the twentieth century are just beginning to realise the importance of film. A great step forward was taken in 1980 when the NHMF recognised its importance to our national heritage. Since then the NHMF has made available to the British Film Institute grants totalling over £500,000.

PHOTOGRAPHIC ACKNOWLEDGEMENTS

We are very grateful to the lenders for providing photographs. We would also like to thank the following:

Keith Barley **18a**
The Bridgeman Art Library **45**
British Aerospace **4**
Cambridge University Collection (Crown Copyright/RAF Photograph) **5**
Christie's **21** (p. 51)
Courtauld Institute of Art **105c**
Curtis Lane & Co. **68**
Giudici-Martin **19**
Harrison Hill Ltd. **18c**
Imperial War Museum, Department of Photographs **8d**, **12** (p. 39), **13** (p. 39), **16**
Ian Lyle **69**
Macclesfield Heritage Centre and Silk Museum **110** (p. 159)
Mansell Collection **115** (p. 169)
The Master and Fellows, Magdalene College, Cambridge **28** (left)

Museum of Antiquities of the University and the Society of Antiquaries of Newcastle upon Tyne **26**
National Maritime Museum **112**
The National Trust: R. W. Davis (**p. 6**), Andrew Haslam **87** (pp. 17, 122), **87a**, **87b**, Mark Feinnes **89** (pp. 127, 128), Mike Williams **89** (p. 129), **110** (p. 162), Ken Shelton **92** (p. 133 bottom)
Natural History Photographic Agency **63** (p. 91)
Quarry Bank Mill **110** (p. 161)
Richard Pearce **23**
Antonia Reeve **37**
Simon Rice-Oxley **17** (pp. 43, 44, 45)
Royal Commission on the Ancient and Historic Monuments of Scotland **110** (p. 160)
Royal Institute of British Architects **73**
Royal Society for the Protection of Birds, Michael Richards **63** (p. 21)
Sotheby's **61** (p. 87), **99**
The Tunnicliffe Trustees © **71** (pp. 98, 99)
Wellcome Institute Library, London **72**

INDEX